On Death and Dying Well

By

Cricket Webb

On Death and Dying Well

Copyright © 2019

All rights reserved. This book or any portion thereof may not be reproduced or used in any manner whatsoever without the express written permission of the publisher except for the use of brief quotations in a book review.

ISBN: 9781697506037

Warning and Disclaimer

Every effort has been made to make this book as accurate as possible. However, no warranty or fitness is implied. The information provided is on an "as-is" basis. The author and the publisher shall have no liability or responsibility to any person or entity with respect to any loss or damages that arise from the information in this book.

Publisher contact

Skinny Bottle Publishing

books@skinnybottle.com

Introduction

I realize that the topic of this book may bring about many differing opinions, but this is, of course, my opinion and my interpretation. I fully believe everything that I have written in the following pages.

I feel everyone has the right to die with dignity and for me that means dying without being hooked up to machines to keep me lying in a bed, so my family can come to watch me wither away and draw up into a fetal position over the years or however long it takes for me to die from some other affliction.

It is pointless to put my family through such agony, it is a drain on the healthcare system, it is a drain on the insurance system and all for futile efforts for the family to come in and see my face but know that I am not really there.

Yes, I know there have been stories of people waking up from comas after 16 years. I have heard them all, but we never get the full story. Most of them find out that their significant other has moved on in life and divorced them and married someone else. While some of them face many years of rehabilitation for all the muscles that have wasted away while lying in their bed. Some of them must deal with severe memory loss and may not know anyone they used to know. Who, in their right mind would want to live for any of that? Certainly not I.

At the same time because of my religious beliefs, I cannot even begin to think about checking out early because I want to avoid the pain that "might" be associated with my dying.

Whatever you think about death I hope this book enlightens you to what actually happens in the dying process, what others think when they know death is imminent, what the Bible says about death and heaven, what others who have said they visited heaven have to say and most of all that death really is nothing to fear.

Chapter 1

What Is It About Death That We Fear?

When I was a child, I was so frightened about death. I was scared and shaky every time we went to a funeral home. I was afraid if I got too close to the casket that I might catch what the corpse had that caused them to die. I mean, think about it, when you are little, that is how your mind works. Isn't that the way your mind worked when you were small?

I was ten when I lost the world's most perfect grandmother. She is the grandmother that everyone else wants their grandmother to be like. She had been sick since August, and they had taken something out of her head called a tumor, but as a kid, I thought she was going to get better. She had been to the doctor, and they had done something called surgery, and I knew my dad, and my grandpa had been away from home for a long time that summer to be with grandma while she was in the hospital. I did not understand malignancy, nor that it was the size of an orange would have anything to do with it.

I concentrated on her getting well. I willed it with all my being. She was MY perfect, precious grandma; always there with open arms and ready with a hug.

I helped her with her physical therapy every day after school and my brother, and I worked with her on her reading. Since no one had explained malignancy to us, we thought she was getting better to be 'grandma' again. I loved her more than any word could explain. We lived about ¼ mile down the country road from her house. My brother and I would bike back and forth to her home several times a day, and no matter how many times we came into her back door she acted like she had not seen us in months. She always had fresh cookies baked and in the cookie jar. Her house was always filled with the aroma of fresh-baked cookies or bread and clean laundry. I can still remember her hugs and the affection you felt when she put her arms around you to pull us close to her heart.

By early January, she was dead. What was dead? They said that she had taken her last breath, but her heart continued to beat for quite some time afterward. That was my first recollection of the word 'dead' and my first experience with losing someone I loved so dearly that I can remember.

I remember everyone crying, but when I saw her in the casket, I still did not comprehend the word 'dead.' No one was explaining dead to me. It looked like she was sleeping. But then they took her box, what I know of as today "the coffin," and put her in the ground and covered her up and I finally grasped that I was not ever going to see her again. I was overcome with as much sadness as a child could be at that age. I was sick to my stomach, and I did not know how to express it to anyone. My father, overcome with grief because he was the youngest of the children was very close to his parents was taking it hard, and he knew that his father would not feel like going on after losing grandma.

Six years later, when I was sixteen, her husband, my grandfather did pass away. He, like her, was the world's greatest grandfather. It was his heart, he had been suffering from congestive heart failure and had kept it hidden from the family for quite some time. I was at the hospital the night before he died.

My Dad said he had been talking to people who had been dead for a long time. If only I had known then of the things I know now, that would have brought me great comfort. I realize now that his loved ones that were on the other side of Jordan were beckoning him home.

He knew he was in the beginning birth pains of dying that night. He stopped producing urine. He told my Dad that 'this is it, it is all over now.' Do I think he was afraid of dying? I feel certain that he was not. I am sure he was ready to join Grandma. I am confident she was waiting for him inside the pearly gates, and I am sure he could see her there waiting for him.

Grandpa had done so much in his life, he had traveled the entire world and worked hard since he was ten years old. As a matter of fact, he had been on his own since he was ten.

He left this world with a family that loved him, but he had been so unhappy since grandma had passed away. He had told my father that he had no more business being on top of the ground than a mole.

This time I knew what death meant, and I cried out in anguish when I heard the news that he was gone. I was angry and did not know who I was mad at because my grandfather who was so unique to my brother and me, and the grandpa we spent time with every day, was gone forever.

Grandpa was the patriarch of our family, so wise and knowing as my father is now. He was a fantastic man, and his family was so dear to his heart. How could he be dead? I wanted to die too, to go wherever he was going. I knew I could not stand to live on this earth without my grandfather. Everyone was grieving, but no one realized that my heart had broken in two pieces and the grief I was feeling was insurmountable. I had to work through it myself. I had a lot of unanswered questions.

Then, at the age of 21, my brother died in a plane crash on December 22nd. When given the news I thought I would never again be able to take a deep breath. I not only felt it for myself but for my parents who had just lost their only son. I was numb and could not think.

We had just spoken at length the night before after our church Christmas play. He told me of his plans to fly with three other young men the next morning but, planned on being back Christmas Eve. It was the absolute, worst experience so far; I had had with death.

It surpassed everything I had felt five years earlier with grandpa. My heart felt like it was coming out of my chest and the type of pain I felt in my heart was so very real that I cannot explain it. It felt like I had a heart attack.

I drew into a cocoon of my making for about six months before I felt I could start to come out of the shadows. I did not want to come out even then, but knew I had to face others whether I wanted to or not; I wanted to stay home and never see the light of day. Even then there was such agony inside me.

At twenty-one, I knew full well what death was as I met it head-on and I did not like it. It just did not seem fair that someone so young and loved by so many had died in the prime of his life. He had only just begun to live.

All four of the boys in the plane stepped out onto eternity at the same time. All their watches had stopped at the exact minute and hour. The impact of when the plane hit the tree line that they could not see in the pre-dawn hours early that December morning was so forceful that it not only stopped all their watches, but it also ripped the central aorta out of the pilot's heart.

The impact alone provided sudden death, and none of them should have ever felt a thing, and the last thing they probably knew or heard was the sound of the plane's wings hitting tree limbs. That is what my mind hopes anyway every time I drift back to that morning which is almost every day.

The plane itself, being ripped to pieces had to be hauled off for the full FAA investigation to identify what had caused the plane to lose altitude. The FAA conducted their study, which seemed to take forever for the final report to be released. There was a crack in the propeller of the plane that could have only been visible if there were an x-ray taken before take-off; that had caused them to lose altitude that early December morning.

I can hear clearly in my mind each of the boys as they were encouraging the pilot, their friend, that he 'had this' and could glide the plane down on that vast open field where they were in southeast Missouri. And, they could have done so, except for that small thin line of trees that got in their way on that dark morning right after take-off.

Do I think they were scared? It was my brother's first flight in an airplane. I somehow do not see him as being afraid. He was always ready for the next adventure. I feel confident, knowing my brother, that he thought that the pilot would glide the plane in just fine. So, I do not think he was scared.

Death of a loved one always leaves those left behind wondering. Wondering what their last moments were like. Did they suffer? Did they cry out for anyone? Did they wish they had stayed home? Did they wish they had some last words they had said to someone?

Those who die a slow death and not a quick, tragic death have time to say their goodbyes to everyone and right their wrongs before leaving everyone behind. Tragic death is faster for those who die, and the suffering is much shorter than those who linger for months wishing for death. Begging for mercy that God let them be free of this earthly body that torments them until they think they cannot stand it any longer.

My grandmother always said that living troubles were worse than dead troubles. As I have grown older, I have come to acknowledge what a wise statement she made. Such a wise woman, if she could only have lived longer and I could have learned more from her.

I look back at my grandmother and grandfather's passing and then at my brother's tragic death and see the abnormality of the fact that dying young is in fact not the natural order we expect of life. At least it is not what I see as the 'natural order.' Grandma and Grandpa's life was following the natural order of the way life should be, but not when the young who have barely started to live, who die, that does not seem to be the natural order. Ecclesiastes 7: 2 says: "death is the destiny of every man." It could not be truer of course as all the words found in the Bible have proven to be true. No one born into this world has ever been exempt from death.

I still do not know how we got through that first year. Every day we got up, it felt like there was concrete on our feet and we could not move forward, but somehow, we did. It was an effort to smile to anyone about anything. Nothing was funny anymore.

Part of my heart was missing. I had worked alongside my brother all our lives on the family farm. We had played together in the house, out in the yard and just as hard as we had played, we had fought, like brothers and sisters always do.

I was the big sister. I was the oldest, the bossy one, the one who spoke for him when someone else asked him a question; as he was the quiet one. When he did say something, everyone stopped to listen as it would mean something. My constant prattling never meant much of anything. I talked all the time about everything.

Even though I had been a Christian for eleven years, I was still immature in my Christianity. Not saying I would not have been any less depressed, but I would have handled everything much differently and been able to realize I would be seeing him again and how quickly time would pass. Even now, in my mind, it seems like it was only yesterday as the entire three days are burned so deeply in my mind. The people, the faces, the words of comfort, seeing my brother for the first time in the casket; all the horrors of facing my denial.

As my parents reached the age of sixty and they were making out their will, I would become distraught, and I could not discuss the fact, nor did I want to hear what their plans were. I would start crying and have to leave the room. I could not deal with the concept of their death after losing my only sibling.

It upset me so much about the thought of them dying. I could not imagine my life without them. I was suffering from anticipatory grief more than I could understand. I am sure it had a lot to do with losing my brother so early, but my brother, parents and I were a close unit as we had all worked side by side on the family farm until I moved away after high school for higher education.

My father, who was always so patient with me, would tell me in the calmest voice, death had been and would always be an inevitable part of life, and at one time or the other, everyone will experience it whether we want to or not.

That I would find out that the older you get, the more natural it will seem and the less you will fear it. I thought that sounded utterly crazy. He could not know what he was saying. Besides, how could I possibly go on without my parents?

But, the older I have become, it is evident to me, and I have found his statement to be so wise; that I have no fear of dying. But I still did not want to talk about their deaths and haven't been ready to buy a ticket for the bus ride to heaven just yet. I know that if I were to die today, I would face no fear whatsoever as I would be going to a place better than where I am now.

Every time my parents now discuss the fact that one day they will die, and they act like it is nothing to be frightened of, I understand what they are saying, but it still upsets me thinking about them not being here. As you age, you no longer have any fear of death as it is a natural part of life.

During my research for this book, I find it is a universal thought that when you are younger, the concept of death is frightening for everyone but as you age and especially when you reach your 70s, 80s, and 90s that the fear is no longer fear but a welcomed relief. The world changes so much from the time when you were born, and you feel that technology has passed you by no matter how hard you have tried to keep up with it that you feel lost and no longer fit in no matter how hard you try.

You start to feel you can't always connect with your grandchildren and great-grandchildren even though they love you to death. You think it is time to say, "I have had a good run, and I have enjoyed it while I was here, but I am tired and more than ready for a promised rest and to see the loved ones that have gone on before me."

Now, that I have gotten older and have had three near-death experiences, the last one being the closest call, I have no fear whatsoever of dying. I have no mountains that I feel I must climb, no sights that I must see, or any significant feat that I must accomplish. I will enter my eternal resting place just as I am.

I am ready to step out onto Eternity whenever God calls me. I now look forward to that day. I have lived well on this earth and done all I need or desire to do, and I have messed up a lot along the way. I have had to ask for forgiveness more times than I like to admit. But at least I serve a God that will forgive me. I have been washed with the blood of the Lamb.

I have witnessed death, and I must admit, God can even make dying a beautiful symphony. People grieving at the time of watching their loved ones pass away do not realize how perfect God makes the death experience. How beautiful it really can be when someone is dying. Please do not think that I am a morbid person because I am not. I am just the opposite. I am a medical person who realizes how unique God designed our bodies. Dying can be as beautiful as the birth process if one allows themselves to accept it as that.

Medical studies can now prove that the soul stays in the body for a period after death before it leaves the body. Never again will I leave my loved ones after the doctors have pronounced them dead until I feel their soul has crossed over Jordan. I am sure their soul will know I am still there.

Physicians who have taken part in this study have been amazed at the discoveries they have made, and they must admit that there has to be a higher power after seeing this phenomenon. Physicians who had been taught to think differently and had never before believed in a higher power that was a part of this study have changed their minds and must admit that indeed, there is a God over our universe.

There has been so much hype in the past about Dr. Kovorkian and how he in the past helped others to die that was terminally ill. What the majority of people seem not to understand is that when we give consent for the ventilator to be unplugged, we permit the doctors to go ahead and help our loved one to pass away. The staff keeps pushing the morphine until the patient's heart stops.

Yes, it is correct, they are keeping them from suffering. But, that much morphine is also slowing the respiration rate and slowing the heartbeat until the heart itself stops and the patient is considered clinically dead.

Many people think that what the doctor or nurses have told them, "We will make sure they are comfortable" is true when it is hastening their death by the morphine stopping their body functions.

My thought on this fact is that our government is to blame for this methodology. To hurry this person along, so they no longer take up space, no longer cost Medicare money (government dollars that patient has paid into during their lifetime), and no longer will require a monthly social security check. Make it stop as soon as possible, please. At this point they are no longer valuable to our society and are just taking up space, so get rid of them as quickly as possible. They are no longer contributing to the community. They are considered a costly burden for our country at this point.

Pure and absolute death is when the brain is considered dead. "Brain Dead" yes, that is what most doctors call it. When you reach this state, most doctors will tell you there is no coming back. But there are those cases when people have come back. It has been very rare, but it has happened.

Tell me, if you were to die right this minute, would your affairs be in order? Would you want to die a long drawn out illness or would you prefer a tragic end? Would you be scared that the tragic ending would be painful or that the long drawn out illness would be painful? Would everything be organized enough for your loved ones that it would not cause them difficulties after you pass?

Chapter 2

What It Feels Like to Be at Death's Door

Like I told you, I have been near Death's Door three times, and the last time I was knocking on the door itself and even had it cracked open.

The first time I was at Death's Door was when my heart was flatlining, and I was in the ER. They had pulled the crash cart to my bedside, as my potassium had bottomed out due to a drug I had been prescribed for pericarditis. I felt like I was floating. Not above my bed or anything like that, but just floating. I felt so very calm and so at peace, with not a worry in the world.

But, I started to hear screaming, and that brought me back to the here an now, as I recognized it was my daughter's voice saying, "Momma, don't die now, I still need you. You can't die now." I came back to the present and felt so ill. I told her I was so sick and did not know if I could go on.

She kept begging, and the crying from my only child is what made me try to hang on, and with her belief and prayers for me, I did hang on and went to ICU for a few days before going to a step-down unit and then home.

The second time that I was nearing Death's Door was when I was so ill with Clostridium difficile. Having Common Variable Immune Deficiency caused me to be very susceptible to this organism taking over my intestinal tract. The abdominal pain felt like a knife going through my gut all the time. The diarrhea was so intense that I was losing 20 pounds a week. I had no appetite. I was losing muscle mass and getting thinner than I had been in years. I know I looked terrible.

I saw myself in the mirror every morning and knew what looked back at me. I was exhausted and felt I could not go on and my legs did not want to hold me up. When I would go to sleep at night, I was sure I would not awaken the next morning. It seemed an effort even to breathe. I was not allowed to be alone at any time during a 24 hour period. That is the only way I could stay home and not be in the hospital. They had me on medication for the c. Diff. but it sure was taking its time in getting rid of the bacteria. They had me on IV antibiotics as well as oral antibiotics. My exhaustion could not have been any worse. My entire body was depleted of everything.

When I did manage to get some food or liquid down, it went through my intestinal tract in a matter of minutes. I was sure I was dying and did not have long to live. I reviewed my will and made some changes with my attorneys. I discussed my life insurance and updated my beneficiaries. I spoke with my attorneys to make sure that everything I wanted had been accomplished before I felt at peace.

I planned a very low key, no funeral, graveside service at the time. I left a note telling my daughter where everything was at so she would have no problems in searching for any of it when I was gone. I was ready for death to take me. I was at peace with dying. Once again, it was not my time. The medicine finally started working, and I eventually began to feel a little stronger. The doctor did allow me to start staying by myself during the day, but at night someone had to be with me.

But I would have to say the closest I have ever come to Death's Door was on my way to work on a bright and beautiful Monday morning. I not only came up to Death's Door and knocked on it, I even opened it up a bit and looked inside. I was driving 63 miles an hour in a 55 mile an hour speed zone when a large farm truck pulled out in front of me, and I was only about 50-75 feet from the truck. I knew I could not stop, but the natural reaction was to slam on my brakes. Before impact, I thought of all my family that depended on me so much. I knew God had a plan.

Looking at the large truck and thinking about the size of my car I could see no way I would live through an impact of this nature. I said out loud that 'today Lord I will see you in Paradise.' I was confident of that fact right before impact. Even though I had buckled in tightly, I was still thrown all over the car. My head was hitting against everything. I felt pain mainly on my head during all the crunching of metal and the explosion of all the airbags. I kept wondering when death would come. Would my head injuries slowly black me out? I couldn't breathe right; it was painful everywhere when I tried to take a breath.

Finally, everything was the quietest I had ever remembered in my life. I no longer felt any pain anywhere on my body. I had to be dead. I wasn't sure what was going on at this point. I guess I had blacked out for a bit. I started coming to enough that people were talking to me but I could not hear what they were saying.

The EMS folks told me my skull was crushed in and that I would be flown by helicopter elsewhere. I argued with them that it was not possible that I had a crushed skull. I did not see double and could speak plainly. They said to trust them; my skull was crushed in on the left side. I only felt calm. No pain at all now. I was at total peace as to what would happen. If it was my time to die, then so be it. I was ready to step out onto the stage of eternity. I was not afraid. Death was just another chapter of life. I have never felt this kind of calm and serenity in my entire life. I was not worried about anything, and I knew that my life was in God's hands.

In the ride inside the ambulance on the way to the hospital, I prayed to God to prepare my daughter to step up to take care of my parents as I had been doing, to take care of her Aunt Chris and Uncle Clint because they had no children and no one to take care of them. They would all need her badly. I didn't feel perfect, but I had worked hard keeping notes on everyone over the years of all their health problems so when I met with their doctors, I could do my very best to help them get the best healthcare possible.

When I got to the Emergency Room, my 78-year-old father arrived almost immediately. How had he come so quickly from 26 miles away? My daughter met me at the ER doors with another RN friend of mine who worked in the ER. Everyone around was my co-workers, and they all looked worried. I had no idea I looked so terrible. There was a lot of whispering, and I was in and out of sleep. My daughter told me they had to take me to a trauma center 180 miles away because they could not treat my injuries at the facility where we worked. I let her know I understood. The next three days, my life was nothing but a blur, and I was in and out of consciousness. But once again I had escaped death and had not passed through that door.

Most people do not realize how many times a day they come to the brink of death. They have no concept because they do not see behind the scenes into the very tiny cells of their bodies. To understand this, you must realize how uniquely the body is made and designed to work in such harmony.

If you sweat too much while working in the outdoors and your potassium gets too low, your heart can stop beating. But, wait, there are myriads of reasons why the potassium can drop low. The heart usually will not just 'stop.' It may skip a beat or two and then 'BOOM' it is over with and if someone is not near that knows how to give CPR; you need to be ready to 'go to the light.'

You are in your shower and have a severe pain hit you in your foot. You have never had a pain like that in your foot before! It is enough that it brings you to your knees. Little known to you but that was a blood clot passing through those tiny veins in your foot and lucky for you, for some reason did not make it to your brain. One of those "ischemic" clots. Where did it come from and why? You are lucky this morning. You did not knock on Death's Door. You didn't even ring the doorbell!

You have just taken a shower and step out to towel off and drop in the floor from a massive stroke. You never regain consciousness, and the doctor's tell your family you are brain dead. They say to your family that they should unplug your ventilator and they will keep you comfortable as you take those last steps out onto Eternity. How can the doctors say something like this to the family and the doctors never have a tear in their eyes or seem to act like robots at this time? Have they become numb to feelings of those who are still saddened by the death of loved ones?

Your son is playing basketball, and he is the teams lead player. He is on fire tonight and making basket after basket. The crowd is wild. He runs over at the end of the quarter, sits down on the bench, talks to the coach and falls onto the floor dead. He has had an unknown congenital heart defect since birth that no one ever picked up on, and tonight it reared its ugly head. He stepped out on to Eternity that night while he was on fire playing basketball on the court and his adrenaline had kept him going until he sat down by the coach.

I know of a beautiful Christian family that their father and husband were dying from congestive heart failure. As he lay dying in his hospital bed, he kept looking toward the ceiling with his family at his side to be with him as he was about to take his last breath. The family could hear singing that sounded like it was out in the hallway. It seemed to sound like a church choir singing gospel hymns. The entire time the patient kept looking up with his eyes fixed on the ceiling as if he was focused on something no one else could see as he drew his last breath. The singing stopped when he quit breathing. The family found out later there was no one singing in the hallway before he died. They all felt sure it was the angels singing him home.

I feel confident that most agnostics and atheists would scoff at most of my stories. What I do know is the day of my salvation and the weeks leading up to it and what I experienced. I feel sorry for those who do not believe in God and His existence and His son who did die on the cross at Calvary for our sins.

Maybe those who profess to be agnostic or atheist should investigate the entire history and story of the Bible and try to disprove the existence of God and Jesus. I know they cannot if they examine it with an open mind and an accurate investigative approach with truth and honesty.

I worked with a nurse who as a child worked for years in the fields of Mexico around all the chemicals they sprayed on the crops during a time that no one was protected against the effects of such. She started to feel very ill, and her liver was found to be hardened, and she turned yellow over her entire body. She developed varices in her esophagus that she did not know existed until one day when she began vomiting up blood and continued to do so until she bled to death. But she knew her Lord and Savior and I know where she is today and that I will see her again.

Your back has been bugging you for a while now, and you keep going to the chiropractor, but it doesn't seem to be helping. Finally, you go to see a medical doctor who sends you to a specialist. You have waited so long because it was just back pain. You find out you are in end-stage pancreatic cancer that has metastasized to the bone and everywhere else in your body and there is nothing that they can do about it.

You are 37 years old and the picture of health. You have three young boys you will not see grow up, a beautiful wife, and one sister you will be leaving behind. But, you love the Lord with all your heart and all your soul. You are a youth pastor at a local church and have affected so many lives. You choose to go home and be with your family for your last days so you can be with your wife and three boys so they can see how a Christian man faces his last days on earth before going home to be with the Lord. At this point, there is no quality of life. In four short weeks, you step out onto the stage of Eternity. And it all started with back pain. Just back pain.

A young mother is giving birth to her first baby. Just as she is heaving that last big push, she goes into severe convulsions and starts foaming at the mouth. Her family is present when this happens. She is dying in front of their eyes, and there is no saving her. She has passed an amniotic embolism. Not as rare as you would think. Per the National Health Institute, there is amniotic embolism of one per every 20,646 births with a mortality rate of 26.4%. Not predictable in the least and not preventable. The young mother stepped out onto Eternity that night leaving behind her newborn for her family to raise.

A young man of law enforcement just recovering from a tonsillectomy is three days post-op and already home from this simple procedure starts to have difficulty breathing. His wife races him to the hospital that performed the procedure. He dies from a pulmonary embolism shortly after reaching the hospital due to a complication from one of the most simple surgical procedures performed. Because of this simple procedure, he stepped out onto the stage of Eternity to be with his Lord and Saviour. He left three small children and a wife; and little known to him or his wife; she is pregnant with another child.

His whole life was a witness for Christ. He lived it every day. His death left everyone reeling that knew him. He was so healthy, and his life was so full of energy and happiness, and he had such a beautiful family to go home to and children to raise. Death by a pulmonary embolism from a procedure such as he had is very rare indeed. But his day and time to go home had come no matter how it was going to happen.

Was he afraid to die? I can assure you he was not scared to die. He was the kind of person that would have worried about how his family would get by after he was gone, but at the same time would have never feared death as he knew his Lord and lived his life every day to serve his God.

I know an elderly gentleman who was very active in his garden and yard and always working. He was mowing his yard when he fell dead. No warning, no prior symptoms, nothing. He had a ruptured abdominal aneurysm. Right there on the lawn, he stepped out onto Eternity.

A forty-year-old man goes in for a heart cath. No big deal, just a simple heart cath. The minute the dye is injected; he codes. No bringing him back. He had stepped out into Eternity.   He leaves a wife and two almost-grown daughters. He was the best man at my brother's wedding. He is still so young; a heart cath should not have been a big issue for someone like him. They say he was allergic to the heart cath dye.

A 50-year-old RN gets up during the night and tells her husband she does not feel well and goes into the bathroom to vomit. She falls dead on the bathroom floor. She has ruptured an abdominal aneurysm she never knew existed and of which she had never exhibited a symptom. She stepped out onto Eternity that night right in front of her husband.

Most of these stories are about people who had no idea they were about to die. They had no idea that the most intricate parts of the way their body worked had deceived them and let them down at just the wrong time.

But there is still no reason to fear death even if anything you do brings the end so much closer. You should live life in 'the moment' every minute, of every day so that you have not wasted any of the precious time you have been given while living on this earth.

The human body is impressive in the way it has been made and designed, and some of the things that happen to it will astonish you so much that it is hard to believe. Each part of our body internally and externally depends on all the other parts.

The inception of a baby being conceived and through its nine months, until it is born, is such an incredible scene to behold. It is indeed a miracle.

At the same time as someone leaves this earth, it is a miracle to behold as well. Dying is a beautiful symphony if you can look past your grief and to the dying process of your loved one.

I knew a little 94year old woman who was a real southern Christian lady who took three days to die. They were sure every day that she would be 'going home.' She had suffered from Alzheimer's for the past four years which complicated her problems even more. She was no longer the fine kept lady who always had on her makeup and the proper jewelry that matched her outfit every day.

On her third day of being in a comatose state where she just lay there making not a sound with her core body temperature not even that of a living human being, no one could believe she was still classified as living. They could not understand how she still had a heartbeat, even though it was down to twenty-four beats per minute. How could she be alive? Bless her heart. Out of nowhere, shocking everyone, she sat up in her bed and spoke to her nephew! She lay back down on her bed, and in a matter of minutes, she stepped out on to Eternity where awaited her a well-deserved rest. It seems that there are some things not meant for us to understand.

A friend of mine had a baby boy that she placed in his baby bed for the night at his bedtime. She covered him with a light blanket. During the night she goes in to check on him, and he is found dead, of crib death. There still has not been a specific reason as to why this happens. A perfectly healthy baby boy with no problems and who has passed all his checkups with flying colors is dead. The angels carried him to Eternity that night. His parents are left to deal with this most horrible tragedy of their little family.

Chapter 3

What If You Are Given a Terminal Diagnosis?

At first, it is such a shock that you don't believe it, and you think it has to be some sick joke. But as you look at the doctor, you realize he is not kidding. Everyone is looking at you and wondering how you are going to take it. Should you joke about it? What are you feeling at that very moment?

You are so overcome with so many emotions that it is hard to define all of them. The first thing you want to know is "How long do I have?"; "How could this be happening to me?"; "Who will take care of my children?"; "Who will take care of my elderly parents?"; "Who will watch over my wife of 62 years?"; and the list goes on forever of the things that run so quickly through your mind.

Whether you are young or middle age; it hits you hard like you have been punched in the stomach. If you happen to be older, say in your 60's you feel sad when the doctor gives the diagnosis, but you realize you have had a good life and can accept the jolting news better than your family can take it.

You will notice that the doctor expresses no feelings whatsoever. So what, another patient is going to die. What is the big deal? It is just one more we can't save. I could guarantee you if it were someone in his family it would be a different story. He would be finding the best doctor in the country who specialized in that type of cancer or disease to try his level best that day to save his loved one. The shoe is on the other foot now. I have seen this happen.

We go through life so many times and take so much for granted. We take chances every day; we do not take care of our health, we do not appreciate the life around us every day.

It seems we all get so caught up in material things and what money can buy. All of the "things" we have accumulated in this life we will not be taking with us when we leave this earth. When we get caught up in this dirty mission, we forget to live and when I say live "I mean to live in the moment" and enjoy each minute as much as we can as it could be our last even if we do not have a terminal diagnosis.

Life is so fragile, as I explain later in the book and every minute is so precious, and we know it can be as unpredictable as a tornado. We need to realize that when we awaken each morning, we need to be thankful we have had the chance to wake up one more time because time is a gift. It has never been a right.

When that terminal diagnosis is given, you think back over the years, especially if you are a woman and think about all the time you spent in the "Salon." To get that perfect cut or color and all the time you spent experimenting with different makeup; and why? That will not be the things that are important when your time has come, and your number is up.

If you are a complainer, stop it. Be happy, be grateful for the things you complain about because you can do them. Don't complain about the things that you do have; God can take them away in a heartbeat.

We take for granted that the day after tomorrow will come; but not with a terminal diagnosis we can no longer assume that will happen. When someone you love has been diagnosed as terminal, and they have three to four months to live, and it is his or her birthday, what kind of present do you get them? Let that soak in for a minute. It brings tears to my eyes.

It is like a kick in their face. What is there to celebrate? Yes, they have had one more year, but you both know there will not be another year and it is immensely depressing.

It's been suggested by one young lady that was diagnosed with a terminal illness that we should give more time to all the people we love instead of buying "stuff" for ourselves that we probably don't need in the first place.

Stress is highly overrated if you ask me. If everyone could quit stressing and worrying so much and think about the good parts of his or her life and concentrate on "the moments," they would be so much happier, and at the end, they would feel so much more fulfilled.

Chapter 4

What Is There To Fear About Dying?

Nelson Mandela once said, "Courage is not the absence of fear, but the triumph over it."

Why do most people fear to die? I think that most people fear death because they fear 'the way they will die' and that there will be terrible suffering that goes with it. They could be right. But, 98% of the time, they will be very wrong.

There is not one of us that has any idea as to how, when, or where we will die. It is all a vast guessing game left up to our Creator. That is my belief. Some of you may have different ideas about this concept, however.

I always worried about being shot to death and how terrible an end that would be and the pain I would endure. Working in the medical field as I have for so many years I have had the privilege to talk to many gunshot victims, and every one of them has told me the same story.

They never knew they had been shot. Each one told me that they never felt it nor realized they had been shot until they either saw the blood or felt the stickiness or wetness of the blood. But, there was never any pain. If they lived from the gunshot, the pain was from the doctors operating on them and probing around their insides to repair what had been damaged by the bullet or shell.

When I say all of this I am not talking about a flesh wound, I am talking about a gunshot wound through the abdominal cavity, through a leg that broke a bone, or through a shoulder blade.

When I see people on TV acting like they are hurting from a gunshot immediately, I laugh to myself a bit as I have talked to so many patients who have all told me the same stories.

For those who are hit in a major artery and bleed out quickly, they usually get confused, short of breath, feel tired and well, go to sleep; but still, they never feel any real pain from the bullet itself.

I feel confident that God causes us to go into a semi-state of shock so that we do not feel pain for a while. The same type of shock that a rabbit goes into when a fox catches it for lunch.

Maybe some fear death because of the way they lived their life. Even if they do not believe in a God of sorts, they still dread the thought of a heaven or a hell or just being put into the dirt and covered up and what lies beyond for them afterward.

Some people never think about what happens to them after they die until they are dying and then become terrified of where they are going. Those people are probably on the road to hell. They have more than likely never accepted Jesus as their personal Savior. If not, they are looking straight at the fires of hell. Those people will usually die with a frightened look on their face and not that of peace as Christians do.

As people age, they seem to value life more, and I find they start to live in the minute more than ever. For example, when I visit with my parents, which is every day, when I begin to leave, my dad always says, "What are you hurrying off for?" I always say, "Dad I have been here a couple of hours." He responds back, "It seems like you just got here." He means it. He lives in the moment all the time now. When he was younger, he worked from daylight to dark making a living for his family. First, as a farmer and then as an owner of a construction business.

Maybe it is because they don't have that much time left and most of them have done or accomplished all they have wanted in life. If not, maybe they have come to concede that even if they didn't achieve all they had set out to, in the beginning, it would not have made that much difference.

When you get older, it seems you appreciate the minutes more. I love the moments with my parents. I still learn a lot of valuable lessons from them as they are now eighty-two years old and they have so much knowledge with all they have been through in their lives.

I notice now the slippage of memory, and they look to me for answers as it is becoming too hard to make their own decisions. Life just gets hard when you get older.

I can remember I wanted to work in cancer research with my background in medical laboratory science. I felt I could have saved the world if I could help find a cure for cancer. Here I am forty years later, and there is still no cure for cancer. But my career path took me down roads that I never thought possible, and in the long run, I feel I have been able to help more people along the way than I ever could have had if I had gone solely into cancer research, isolating myself into one area of study.

As I look back, I am glad that I did not follow the path of Cancer Research as I would have had to live much farther from the family farm and my family roots. There was something about my upbringing that draws me back to that part of my life that still holds me here, and I am happy to live close now to care for my parents as they age and as my aunt ages.

For the most part, if you were to question anyone in their 80s, 90s or older, I feel confident you would find they would all tell you that they have had a good life. You might find one or two that had a lost love they wish they would have pursued or that if they had put a child up for adoption that later in life were never able to reconnect with, but for the most part, they had a good life.

You will also find that people in this age group are not scared of dying. Some even look forward to it. Why might you ask? If you would talk to them, they would more than likely tell you they are tired of living. All of their loved ones have gone on and the day to day drudgery for them is just too much to bear.

After my perfect grandmother passed, I could not understand why my grandfather lost his will to live. Were we not enough for him? All of his remaining children were still living, and he had 12 grandchildren. Was that not fulfilling enough for him that it would be enough?

Grandpa told my father that without my grandmother he had no more business being above the ground than a mole. He was so lost without her. He lived for six years after her passing, longing for death to take him so he could be with her.

Fear of death in a young adult is understandable as they have their whole life in front of them. They do not want to think about death. There is so much of life they have not experienced. They want to experience young love, they want to experience going to college and having an occupation, they want to experience raising a family and maybe to travel. They may have a whole list of goals they want to accomplish, so they do not want to board the 'death' train right now.

But as you age and experience the good with the bad of life and the years start to bring changes on and about your body, you begin to notice those wrinkles on your face you have never seen before, and what about that gray hair that you are for sure was not there yesterday morning. You happen to look in the mirror and feel confident that the person looking back at you can't be you. That person seems old now.

Then your children are happy to tell you that you have much more gray on the back of your head. Your muscle mass starts to decrease; some develop issues with incontinence which is not fun to talk about but is so right. Your hormone levels decline, your bone density is less, thereby leaving room for hip and other bone fractures.

You must start to look ahead and consider all the things you used to do and be mindful of how you do them and ask for help with some chores you always did for yourself. It bothers you to ask for help because you are an independent person. It becomes necessary whether you like it or not so you do not injure yourself.

Do you do this because you fear death? No. You do this because you fear you will be a burden to someone else if you injure yourself. You do this for the simple fact that you do not want to spend the rest of your life bound to a wheelchair or bedfast. You use common sense to stay as healthy as possible.

I have been around people who fear death. When I say they fear death, I mean they are terrified! They are screaming and doing everything they can to keep from dying. Most of those folks were far from dying but had themselves convinced that they were dying at that very moment.

Some of the people that I know that fear death, even fear to enter a funeral home. These are grown adults in their 60s and 80s. They are Christians. They have always had a fear of death.

Small children who are battling cancer do not fear death when it is imminent. They learn that the angels are waiting and most nurses and doctors who are in attendance with them will tell you that the children can see the angels and they talk to them. No one else can see them, but the child that is dying from cancer can see them and they talk freely to the angels. Most of the time the child knows when the angels will be coming for them and share the time frame with their nurses and doctors. Those children have no fear of death. They only worry that their parents or siblings will be sad.

No, they are not hallucinating by any means. They are the recipients of a gift that most of us will not open ourselves up to because of the tainted minds of aging that keep us from being able to enjoy such an experience. Children are all so innocent and are not suspicious of everything in this world.

There is no reason to fear death when you think about it. Death in itself is not painful. What is distressing is the disease process that leads us up to the point of departure. The disease process itself can be excruciating.

For the elderly, death is usually a painless, effortless process. It is hard for the family to watch as they sit by the bedside holding their hands, waiting for them to cross over Jordan and to step out onto Eternity.

Years ago death was proclaimed when someone's heart stopped beating, or the patient ceased breathing. However, it is now identified today, as once the brain is diagnosed as dead, there is no longer any brain activity.

Maybe you can think of it in this way. As a baby comes into the world, everything that was dependent on the mother is being cut off, and now the baby is born into this world and now is a living breathing being on its own with all its organ systems coming alive and working independently from the mother.

As we are dying, our body parts all start failing us, and they have been wearing out every day we have lived since we were born, no matter how good we take care of ourselves. Eventually, our heart will stop, and we will quit breathing, and without oxygen, the brain will begin to die.

We should be aware however and realize that the brain does not die instantly. It may take minutes to maybe two hours for the mind to cease to live as it is the last thing to die.

Here is an interesting fact. There are actual cases in which people have for whatever reason been beheaded, and their lips kept moving. A lip reader on site is able to read the lips and tell what the head was saying. Laugh you may, but it has happened because the brain had not had time to die at that point.

After your brain dies, the rest of your body will die slowly. By the end of three days, you are just a lump of rotted protoplasm. Your body doesn't matter. What matters is your soul, and it has been proven by modern medicine to live on even after the brain is considered dead.

It is tough for me to fathom why others fear death because of what is promised to us in God's word. It states that at the end of our life we will go to live in a place that is so beautiful, and peace exists like none other we have ever known.   A place where God has gone to prepare many mansions for us to live.

When you look at almost any religion, one of the common threads you will find is that they all believe in an afterlife. They vary in what the afterlife may look like or what lay in store for them in each specific religion, but there is almost always an afterlife.

One specific experience I was involved in that will forever live in my heart and mind as if it were yesterday was at the deathbed of a dearly beloved uncle. He had fallen and broken his hip at his church after the preaching service one Sunday and had to have a hip repair and an unfortunate surgical site infection invaded his body causing him to fall the victim of sepsis. He was in hospital for six weeks.

Being his Durable Power of Healthcare Attorney, he had always made sure that I knew that no matter what, do not let them keep him alive on a ventilator. I had promised him with all my heart that I would abide by his wishes no matter what may happen. Being Power of Attorney for Healthcare is a job that sometimes is one of the hardest jobs you might ever encounter and be responsible for in your life.

During his death, it was like watching a slow symphony. At first, the doctors told us my uncle had congestive heart failure. It was in a man who had never had any problems with his heart. Then we were told his lungs were filling with fluid because his heart was failing. Next, because his heart and lungs were doing so poorly, his kidneys were failing, and we needed to put him on dialysis 'short term.'

Then the doctors called me at my office 3 ½ hours away and said to me that he needed to be on the ventilator. I drove the 3 ½ hours and talked to my uncle and explained we would only try it for a while, and if it did not work then we would not leave it like that, and he agreed that is what he wanted to do. We had talked about this moment so many times since his son died, but I never thought the time would come so soon.

It was breaking my heart. I was watching his body break down a little at a time. What was worse, I was watching my aunt, his little wife of almost 60 years watch him suffer through all of this terrible mess that was not their faults; but the failures of some very ignorant physicians, who, again if it had been their family would have been handled entirely different.

When I would make my 3 ½ hour drive to the hospital, I would cry the entire way there. When I would drive the 3 ½ hours back home, I would cry all the way back again. I cry now as I write this part of the book. I do NOT cry because he died as I know he is with the angels. I cry because I am greedy and because I miss him so very much and I cry because he had suffered enough the last three years he lived from the shingles he had contracted in his eye and on his head and he was not able to read for very long at a time, his favorite past time. It caused such pain for him.

His feet hurt him so badly to walk on them that it was getting unbearable for him to try to walk without a walker. He had injured one during active maneuvers in the reserves while in college and the other he had fallen at the church on the parking lot on black ice a few years earlier.

He was a quiet man. We shared the love of books, history, and our favorite topic was Abraham Lincoln. We were both Abe Lincoln addicts. He was also my "go-to-man" for questions regarding the Bible. His longtime pastor and best friend of 20 years called him the "J Man" at his funeral. The Jesus man. I shall always remember what Pastor Jim referred to him as the Jesus man as my uncle was a quiet man and he was always working for the Lord without any fuss or any complaining.

He was always so careful to manage his diabetes, but with all of this going on with the infection, the diabetes was running rampant. His toes were turning black and pus was running from some of them. His legs were swelling, and even with the dialysis, he was not making urine. His body was giving up on him even though we were not.

The doctors called me and said that it was the time we talked about unhooking him from life support. There was nothing more they had to offer that could help him at this point. I needed to discuss this with my aunt. Another box to check as the hardest thing I ever had to do in my life. While I knew they were right, I also knew that my aunt's life was about to change forever and our family was about to lose a very precious member that would be sorely missed. When the physician called me at work, I felt like he had stabbed me with a butcher knife right in my heart. What I knew inside, that this day was coming, but now it had been spoken into word. It meant that it was time to say good-bye.

My aunt and uncle did not have any living children so at the bedside stood my aunt, two of her sisters, four nieces, a nephew, and my uncle's pastor and his wife in attendance when the extubation was to be carried out.

The nurses said they would make sure he was 'comfortable.' Yes, that was the word they used. In my mind, I knew what they meant, they would give him medication so this can be over quickly for everyone and we can get on with our work, and you will not hear him gasping for breath. I had not been in healthcare for more than four decades and at the bedsides of this same scenario with families to not know what they were not saying.

My uncle's eyes were wide open, and tears were running from the corners of both eyes. I was speaking softly into his left ear and telling him all his suffering was over now and he could go on home and be with his grandma and grandpa that raised him, his mother who had died when he was six months old. I told him he would see his son, Steve that had died eight years earlier and now Steve would be well when he saw him.

I kept wiping the tears from his eyes that stayed focused directly above him. I am confident that he knew what was happening and it hurt me so badly to be doing this; this saying goodbye and ending his life but at the same time abiding by his wishes. This is what I would have wanted if I had been in his place.

After it was over and he had drawn his last breath, it was hard to leave his side. I felt that something, I was not sure what, was holding me there at his bedside. I kept wishing for my aunt's sake I could will him back to life and in perfect health, but looking at him there I knew that all hope for that was gone. His life had been stolen from him one piece at a time.

A few weeks after I had gone back to southeast Missouri, the whole scenario was still bothering me. I was discussing what had happened with my Dad and how the tears kept running from his eyes and the nurses tried to explain them away to me. I knew they were real tears and I was sure that my uncle knew what was happening. The nurse had no idea I worked in healthcare and that she could not make things up to me and I believe what she dished out.

My Dad, always so knowing and calm said, "Did you ever stop to think he was getting a glimpse of heaven and all those who he had been missing?" How selfish of me to have not thought of that. How wise of my Dad to think of it in that way. Dad was probably right, and my uncle was probably seeing his son he was missing so badly that had died eight years earlier, his grandma and grandpa who had raised him, and his mother that had died when he was a baby that he had never even met. What a beautiful reunion must have awaited him at the gates of Heaven! I am so happy for him, but the selfish part of me misses him terribly at times. My aunt seems to be taking it very well at times, but I know she misses her Clint. She is not afraid of dying either. She knows her Clint and her Steve are waiting for her at heaven's gates.

I know of a very dear Christian lady who started having bronchitis symptoms who had been healthy all her life.

She went to her doctor and received the diagnosis of COPD (chronic obstructive pulmonary disease). Chronic, that means a condition that exists over an extended period. She had just become sick, so how could it be chronic? The doctor told her she had about five years to live and explained to her that she might want to use oxygen when she felt she needed it.

Within two weeks, she was having more trouble breathing and went back to her doctor. He told her she had one week to live! She was placed on a ventilator. She called all her children in to say goodbye to them, some living far away, and then she wanted the ventilator to be shut off. She was in control of her death. Her mother, in her 90s, was at her side the entire time. Her little mother's heart was broken. Her mother, also a Christian, but very close to this daughter who lived near to her and watched after her mother every day. The only way the daughter could communicate while on the ventilator was by writing.

All of her children over a week's time came in to see her and visit with her as well as all her grandchildren. She was relieved that she got to see all of her children before having the doctors turn off the respirator. After the last child had made it to the hospital to see her and with her family at her side, she told them she was ready for the respirator to be turned off as she did not want to live her life hooked to a machine.

The machines were turned off; drugs were given so there would be no suffering and she went to sleep forever as she stepped out onto Eternity to be with loved ones that had gone on before her.

Last fall, my best friend lost her husband to a massive stroke from a blood clot passing through his brain. The doctors at the bedside told her and her children that he was more or less brain dead and they could do nothing more. It was the truth, he could not move his right side, and they said he was probably blind, brain dead, and could not speak. My dear friend had to face what to do for her beloved companion who was now on the ventilator because he could not even breathe for himself. She cuddled his head in her arms and cried and told him she did not know what to do as they had always made their decisions together.

This good, Christian, humble man, who was supposed to be brain dead, brought his left arm up and hugged her body and patted her with his hand not once but twice as if to say; you know what to do. We have discussed this many times before. Let me go. You know our faith, and you know where I am going when I leave this world. It is time.

I had a dear aunt that over seventeen years ago was dying of lung cancer and was in a hospital bed at home with hospice. On this particular night, she said to her husband with each gasping breath that for that night she wanted to sleep with him in their bed and not in the hospital bed. He told her whatever she wished would happen. They had not been laying in bed long when, as weak as she was, she began flailing and trying to get up, with his help, she stood up on her knees in the bed and grabbed each of his arms with her hands.

As she did this, she fell backward, dead. Cancer had finally eaten through the main artery, and she had bled to death internally.   It was over for her.   She had suffered so terribly.   She knew something was happening and somehow that day she knew she would die that night and wanted to be with her husband when she died and not lying alone in her hospital bed. My aunt stepped out into Eternity that night. No doubt in my mind. Her battle here on earth was over, and victory was now hers.

Scientists in the United States have proven that the soul lives on even if the brain ceases to function. It is separate from your physical body and your brain. Your soul will continue to exist and at some point will leave your body and go on to your heavenly home. If you are in the room long enough, you can almost feel it as it leaves the body. You will know, you will feel it.

Chapter 5

What Happens To Your Body as We Age and Die?

Experiments conducted over and over show us that our human cells, when grown in tissue culture, can only be divided 50 times, and then they die. There are some exceptions to this, and that has to do with cancer cells, and they never stop growing and invading unless something can be found that will kill them. Our muscle and brain cells never divide again after we are born. There are people like me that wish my brain cells would divide some more as I question if I was born with enough of them.

Some people who are dying and no they have only hours or days to live sometimes voice regrets. Of those regrets, the ones that you hear over and over from everyone at death's door are:

- I kept putting work before my family. I should have dedicated more time to them.

- I wish I had taken the chance and followed my dreams.

- I wish I would have said the words, "I LOVE YOU" many more times.

- I feel I should have made more time for my best friends.

- I should have been less stubborn and said I was sorry.

- I wish I would have spoken my mind and not held back causing resentment.

- I don't know why I didn't save more money for retirement.

- I wish we had had children; it is so lonely now.

- Being a happy person is something you choose, and I wish I had known that earlier.

- I would have liked to have been brave enough to live a truthful life.

One theory on aging that I tend to agree with is that on wear and tear of growing old and dying; suggests that our genes become altered for some reason and their mutations that seem to aggregate over time and lead down that ugly path to becoming old and lead to death.

Every day we are exposed to some ugly agents in our environment like radiation (how many have not had an x-ray), toxic chemicals (in our drinking water, even the bottled water, in our air), can all contribute to mutating DNA. Our cells know how to repair themselves, but sometimes even the repair mechanisms fail, and the mutations will pile up. This specific failure leads us to believe that it plays a role in cancer developing in individuals.

Free radicals are considered to contribute to aging. The best way to block these free radicals is the intake of vitamins E and C to retard aging. It seems there are some of us that need all the help we can get.

It seems that somewhere in the 72 hours before death, we know it is going to happen. Most doctors want to tell you that it is just the effects of the drugs they are giving. I, for one, do not believe in any of the hocus-pocus they feed you. In recent studies on deathbed experiences, most patients who were still conscious at least an hour before dying could tell you they saw deceased family members beckoning them to cross over, and this was even with patients who were not medicated.

One patient who we will call Audrey who lay dying of cancer said her son Frankie kept coming by to see her. Frankie had been dead for several years. She kept telling everyone he was sitting over there in an armchair in the room.

There have even been cases that dying patients see some of their family or friends that they did not even know had died. In one case, a young mother giving birth to her baby told her doctor that her Father was at the foot of the bed and he has Vida with him. Vida was her sister who had died three weeks earlier, and they had not told the young mother about the death.

There is the story of the father who died abruptly. The family had no warning, the father had not been sick, but in the middle of the night, he just died. His daughter who lived 100 miles away, was awake in her bedroom, all of a sudden felt there was someone near her, and she felt hands holding the back of her head. She felt overcome with a feeling of joy and contentment. The experience was so vivid that she shared it with her son before either of them found out her father had died.

An advertising executive in Toronto was driving on a cold night six weeks after her father had passed and the next thing she knew her Dad was sitting in the passenger seat. He rode with her for a while she stated, and it was an incredibly realistic experience.

Myself, about two weeks after my brother had died in a plane crash he appeared to me. He came to sit on the tailgate of one of his pickups. He said to tell Mom and Dad that he was fine where he was at, everything was ok, where he was he could not see anyone crying, not to worry. It was all going to turn out fine. I told him they were going to be so happy to see him. He said he could not stay long. He wanted me to give Dad two messages (two things I had no idea about). He told me that he had never gotten around to winterizing his water pump for his home and that there was something wrong with the oil "something" on his white tractor. Dad could not figure out what I was talking about until next spring when he started driving the tractor and that part of the tractor went out on him. At this point, I could hear Mom and Dad coming down our gravel road in their truck and asking my brother to please wait to see them as he dissolved into a mist.

I know for a fact that coming from anyone this sounds corny. I do not blame you. But I promise with all my heart I knew nothing about his pump to his house and I sure did not know about the oil system on his tractor. How could I know this if he had not appeared to me?

It seems that in our culture of today, people have a hard time talking about death. It seems the people who are dying know more than what we know about it. We just need to start listening to what they are saying.

When our body is ready to die some signs start to show that indicate to us that the body is in the final stages of preparing itself for a shutdown.

Our extremities will start feeling colder to others' touch, and our skin color will probably change by looking mottled. It is normal and shows that our blood is needed for our organs. Our family may need to add an extra blanket to cover us, but they should never use an electric blanket.

We may start sleeping more and be hard to wake up. Our metabolism is slowing down. Our loved ones need to sit with us and speak softly to us. Do not talk about us when we are right there by you as hearing is the last to go.

We will probably get disoriented and confused about all kinds of things, and that is because of the metabolism change.

As our muscles begin relaxing, we might lose control of our bowel and bladder. Just try to keep us clean and comfortable.

We may start sounding like we are gurgling down from our lungs and it might get pretty loud. It is all because we are not drinking as much and just can't cough anything up now. Suctioning will not do any good and can make it even worse. It will be best to turn us on our side and just let gravity do the work. Just know that this sound is not causing us any pain.

We may start acting restless, and motions may seem repetitive. The oxygen flow to the brain is getting less and less all the time. Don't try to stop us but talk softly or play some soothing music.

You will notice that we are not making hardly any urine and what we do make is very dark-colored. Do not worry as this too is normal.

We will get to where we do not want to eat or drink anything, but let it be as we will have no appetite or be thirsty. You can keep the lips moist, but please do not make us feel guilty for not eating.

It won't be long, and you will notice that the breathing pattern is changing. We may breathe like this for a while, and then begin taking very shallow breaths and then not breathe at all for maybe up to a full minute. Do not be alarmed. We promise this is all part of the "symphony" of dying.

We might start being unresponsive or even appear to be in a coma. It is the beginning of letting go of life here on earth.

We may start talking to loved ones that have gone on before us. That is alright too, the ones we are seeing are probably waving at us to cross on over the River Jordan, and they have a banquet prepared for the feast. Many we have not seen in years. How we long to be with them as there is no pain or fatigue there and everyone looks so happy, that you are about to join them. Better yet, everyone there has their youth back, and they all look like they are in their thirties.

You may notice that we might get a little restless and that could be that something is disturbing us. Just talk softly and tell us it is ok to let go.

At this point, we will probably only want a 'few' certain people by our side. We are ready to say goodbye and making sure you are prepared to let us go.

Please permit us to die. We need to hear it. Do not make us feel guilty and try to keep us here longer. We love you more than you can ever know and will be waiting for you at the gates when you come to enter. They are real, I can assure you of that, the Bible promises it is so. Tell us you love us and say goodbye and see you later. It will be ok if you cry. Tears will express the love you have for us.

You will know we have stepped out into Eternity when we no longer breathe; our heart quits beating, and if our eyelids open, our pupils will enlarge, and our mouth will be slightly ajar. But that is ok too. You can sit with us as long as you would like to say good-bye. Our body may have died, but our soul remains with us for a while, and our brain is still alive no matter what they tell you. Even though the brain may not show any activity on an ECG, the cells inside are still viable and will live on for a while after our heart has ceased to beat, and our respirations have stopped. You can even talk to us. That will be just fine. Our souls will hear you. They like to listen to you speak.

Now after we have ceased to breathe, you will see these things below start to happen. Do not be frightened by any of them. It too is all normal.

When we die, immediately all of our muscles relax, our legs and arms will become flexible, our pupils dilate, and our skin will sag. For some of us, this would not be welcome if we already have sagging skin.

Within mere minutes of the heart-stopping, the skin will no longer look pink because all the blood in the tiny veins in the skin will drain away.

While all the rest of this is happening, the body will start to cool down from 98.6 degrees to whatever the temperature is around the body.

As the body temperature gets lower – two degrees in the first hour and then one degree each hour after that it will give you a timeframe as to when the death occurred.

Since the heart isn't pumping any blood anymore, gravity is going to pull that blood to the body parts closest to the ground. It will cause the body nearest to the ground to turn reddish-purple because the blood is pooling in that area.

About three hours after dying, rigor mortis sets in with it starting in the jaw, eyelids, and neck. It will continue until it spreads over the entire body.

After twelve hours the muscles will all start loosening up in the reverse order that it occurred in the first place.

When you think about the dying process, allow yourself to think deeply about it. Dying is as fascinating as the birth process. Both are like a beautiful symphony that only God himself can orchestrate. I am not mocking anything that has to do with dying. In case you have not noticed, I am mystified by the dying process. No, I am not a morbid person, and I do not rush to the bedside of those who are taking their last breaths. I am just not scared of dying. That too is God's perfect design.

Yes, I do think about what and who I am leaving behind. I think about what my grandchildren will grow up to be and what advice I need to leave them with before I go (not that I am sure I could impart any great words or that they would miss me too much). I think about who will take care of my aged parents and my elderly aunt. I think about my daughter and missing time with her as I know there will be no more family left on our side for her to stay bonded to, so she will need to depend on her boys and their chosen wives and that worries me up to the point that I trust God has a plan.

Then I think about all of us spending our time together in Eternity, and the worry that started to enter my mind leaves as quickly as it would if it had flitted by like a bird in the wind.

Chapter 6

What About Euthanasia?

There is much to think about and a lot to say on this subject, and there is still today much controversy over euthanasia. After all my time studying the idea, I must add that for me, I would not be able to exit life in this manner.

Suicide is not the answer to a problem. There are other paths to walk. God tells us that in His words that the pain we struggle with in life, He will in some way turn it around for us for good. He will use it in such a way that it can strengthen us and others.

Reverend Billy Graham says on speaking about suicide that when he answers questions about suicide, he has to pray very hard that God let him speak the right words, so he does not give encouragement to anyone who is considering suicide. The action of suicide is an action that causes so much pain to all the family that is left behind.

The Bible does NOT say that suicide is unforgivable. There is only one sin that God cannot forgive. That is the sin of a person rejecting God's offer of Salvation in Jesus Christ. If you reject God, then He, in turn, will reject you. There have been cases (such as with Judas) when after he rejected Jesus, he committed suicide.

Only God knows your heart and it is not His will that you commit suicide. It is by His grace we have been saved and not because we are perfect. The Bible states, "For it is by grace you have been saved, through faith" (Ephesians 2:8).

However, I also must admit, that I hate the idea of having to watch my family member die a long, torturous death. Working in healthcare for forty-two years I have seen it all, and no matter how they die, it is sad to those left behind, and for those who die, who are believers, it is the happiest time that they will ever experience, and it will last forever.

Yes, I am a born-again Christian, and I am not afraid to say that I am. In this day and time, that makes me an open target for a lot of people to hate me. But, if I am to be honest about what I write, I must take a stand for what I believe to explain why I feel the way that I do.

The Bible is a history book. It covers a time of over 1600 years. The authors of this divine book were forty total and came from all types of occupations. There were prophets, government officials, fishermen, kings, teachers, shepherds, poets, and peasants. The Bible was originally written in three different languages and on three different continents.

In God's Holy Word, the Bible, you will find that all of us have sinned and there is not one of us perfect even though we call ourselves Christians. I ask for forgiveness every day. I know for sure that I sin every day, and sometimes I am sure I sin and do not even realize it. I am sure I sin by omission. The only person who was ever free from sin was Jesus despite the naysayers who want to mock Him and say things to the contrary. Our salvation is so simple and can be obtained easily by God's grace by having faith in Jesus Christ as your Savior.

Doing good works for others and being kind will NOT get you into heaven. The Bible states this fact. There are many, many people that believe this theory. The only way to heaven is by the blood of Jesus Christ.

The Bible also says that everyone will enter heaven or hell when they die, and it will all depend on whether they have accepted Jesus Christ as their personal Savior. You will not find in the Bible anything about reincarnation, purgatory, or the ending of your soul.

Becoming a Christian is so very simple as all it takes is repeating the sinner's prayer. If you do not know how or what to pray here is all you have to do. When you pray, do so by praying from the bottom of your heart, "Heavenly Father, I am so sorry for my sin, I repent for what I have done! Please have mercy on me! Today, I receive Jesus Christ as my personal Saviour from sin and its penalty. I believe He died for me, was buried, and rose again and I trust today in His sacrifice and the blood He shed for the forgiveness of my sins. Please give me the free gift of eternal life. In Jesus's name, I pray, Amen."

My point is this; even with one of the ten commandments is "Thou shalt, not murder" you will find that some religions do believe in euthanasia for different reasons.

I will try to expound on my thoughts about why my heart feels as it does about euthanasia.

• God, the creator of all, also owns the spirits and souls of all flesh.

• God is the one who has designed a specific time for all of us to die. Ecclesiastes 3:1-2, "To everything there is a season, and a time to every purpose under the heaven: A time to be born, and a time to die; a time to plant, and a time to pluck up that which is planted;" In Ecclesiastes 7:17, "Be not over much wicked, neither be thou foolish: why shouldest thou die before they time?"

• When we die our spirit leaves our body and this in itself is an act of God. Our soul stays on for a while. There is debate as to how long. Some say an hour and some say as long as three days because of Christ arising on the third day. Ecclesiastes 8:8, "There is no man that hath power over the spirit to retain the spirit; neither hath he power in the day of death." Ecclesiastes 3:21, Although animals do not have a soul they do have spirits.

• If we participate in euthanasia, we are ending a life before God's timing. Per God's word, our government is the only authority that can take a person's life, and that is only through Capital Punishment. Exodus 20:13, "Thou shalt not kill," and Matthew 19:18, "Thou shalt do no murder."

- Even if you assist or aid with euthanasia, you are acting as if you are God. In the scriptures, it authorizes physicians that they can treat the pain but nowhere will you find that they can take a life of someone that is dying. Physicians may predict that the person will suffer pain that they may not be able to control. How can they possibly know that for sure?

Aside from God's word about thou shall not murder, there is an oath that all physicians take when they swear in as physicians that is called the Hippocratic Oath. One part of the Hippocratic Oath says, "I will never give a deadly drug to anybody if asked for it, nor will I make a suggestion to this effect." Does anyone not live up to a sworn promise they make any more? Is your word no longer your bond? I would think that the Hippocratic Oath would be one of the most serious Oaths that anyone would ever take since physicians hold lives in their hands every day.

I, for one, think about the financial burden and how if the end of my life should drag on would be such a hardship and wearing down on my family. It makes me sad beyond measure to think that I would be such a burden to anyone as I would never wish to do that.

When you talk to most religious leaders, you will find that by being present to support patients who are terminally ill as they are suffering and at times experiencing fear, you will help them not to choose an early death. Being with them allows their family and friends blessings they never expected to receive during this time nearing the end of their loved one's life.

You will also find those in religious communities that there is something meaningful in caring for a dying person. You learn what each of us will face when our time comes.

It seems that we hear more and more of people who end their own life today is because they cannot afford the medical cost. Our current health care system has become so flawed and broken that to most it seems it will never be any better. The big pharma companies have abused their power so extensively in the United States that most of the seniors cannot afford their medications. Even if they have Part D for prescriptions, they soon fall into the famous 'donut hole.' The senior is stuck there forever, and their co-pays on so many of their drugs are so high they cannot afford them, or their drugs are just not paid by their plan, and there are no other drugs that will work for their condition. They simply have nowhere else to turn.

As seniors are living older and older, we are running into a group that will soon form greater than two million that have Alzheimer's. I do not know what we will do with that many people who have this debilitating disease at the same time. I am afraid the earth will begin to look like the 'Dawn of the Living Dead.'

If you think about it, at times, we are orchestrating when patients die. For instance, if a doctor and the family decides they will not treat pneumonia that has developed in a patient, speeding along the death of someone who has terminal cancer. Or, what if a patient who refuses to eat or drink and they do not supplement them with hydration or protein feedings, hastening their death by starvation.

But, again, in this way, it is the natural course of dying. That is why a living will by the patient is of utmost importance. That way, no one but the patient decides as to what point specific acts are put into motion. If antibiotics are used, if a ventilator is put into place – it will all be called by the patient who made this decision while they were of sound mind.

It is important to remember that religion has always been an essential part of the dying process. It teaches the believers they have a beautiful eternity ahead of them when they leave this world and the dying are comforted by prayers offered up for them as their loved ones surround their death bed.

As firmly as I feel that euthanasia is wrong, there are those who think that it has been provided to them by God. To me, euthanasia seems to be just another means of suicide.

When you look at the numbers of suicide victims, you will quickly find that Atheists and Agnostics have the highest suicide rates of any group that can be found. That could be because Atheists do not believe in any afterlife and often scoff at those of us who do feel that way. I do not mind that they scoff at me. But I do have a real concern for them and their way of thinking.

I can understand someone in the throes of dying and death is imminent in two to three days and they develop pneumonia, to not treat that patient for pneumonia. It makes no sense to prolong their dying by giving them more medicine and needlesticks than must be done for them. There is little chance that it will hasten their death as they are already headed in that direction at a breakneck pace as it is, so letting nature take its course would be dying naturally in my way of thinking.

In the last few years, we have heard more and more about the case of euthanasia. There is one highly publicized case where one young lady at 29 years old that because of the brain tumor she had been diagnosed with, found out she had but a short time to live chose euthanasia when she came to the point when she did not think she could bear it anymore due to the horrendous seizures and she did not want to be a burden to her family.

For the time she had left she did a lot of things she had always wanted to do. To read her full story it brings you to tears.

She chose euthanasia because the physicians told her what the end would be like and she desired to be able to die with dignity in her way of thinking. The morning that she decided that it would be the day, she suffered another terrible seizure. She had decided to take a walk with her husband, came back to their house and went to bed surrounded by her select few loved ones. She had a friend who was a physician that had prescribed for her the pills for her time to die. She took the prescription for her death that her husband had picked up at the pharmacy for her. It only took five minutes, and she was asleep. In thirty minutes, she took her last breath. She was able to leave the world without pain and die peacefully.

Then you read the story of the preacher's wife who died of breast cancer who had four very young children she was leaving behind. She did not choose euthanasia as she felt it was suicide. She said that up to the very last there were some of the most beautiful times and memories she could have left for her children and husband to remember. Once a gorgeous young woman; in the end, you could hardly recognize her cancer-riddled body, but she was still beautiful to her husband and family. The same beautiful spirit still resided in her as always, and she died with dignity.

I look back to years gone by when our forefathers of the Civil War died slowly and agonizingly from their wounds. They screamed out in pain as they died. The only thing they had to help numb their pain was whiskey. Extremities that were cut off as they were bleeding to death and most lay there in the hot sun begging to die.

I know you have watched as many war movies as I have and seen many times when a soldier was dying and in terrible pain and asked his comrade to please finish him off and end his suffering. Was that murder? Was that a form of euthanasia? In my opinion, it was euthanasia. Death was not taking its natural course as they would bleed out in a matter of seconds or minutes and before they bled out, they would have gone into a coma-like state and not have known anything anyway. Why ask your comrade to commit murder?

If I were the dying person on the war front, I can assure you I would be tempted to beg someone to do the same, but also knowing in my heart that I would not be able to ask anyone to finish me off as it would be against my beliefs.

Watching your loved ones die and take their last breath is heartbreaking. Yes, it is also beautiful too. We are heartbroken because we are selfish since we will not see them on this earth again. But, if they have given their heart to God, we will see them in eternity one day if we also have given our heart to God.

If you have a loved one that has always denounced the Lord, Jesus Christ, you know when they draw their last breath that they will live their eternity in a pit of fire and brimstone and begging for a cold drink of water that they will never receive. They will be living in the clutches of Satan. Yes, Agnostics and Atheists, you can make fun of me and call me a deplorable, I am not afraid of you. I stand on God's Holy Word and what it says. His Holy Word was here long before any of us. In case you think it is not important, go back and read about Sodom and Gomorrah and see if that does not remind you of someone you might know today.

We are hearing and reading of more and more people who are coming out and telling of their visits to heaven and of seeing Jesus and God while there. The stories are coming from children who do not even know how to lie and of adults who had experiences as well.

There is a well-known neurosurgeon who before his experience never had an actual religious belief in anything. He had been raised by his parents in a Christian home and had been brought up in the church all his life. His father had also been a neurosurgeon. Eban Alexander had a near-death experience that was brought on by bacterial meningitis that most would not have survived. But, he recovered much to everyone's surprise from being brain dead to being completely recovered and with no traces of any brain damage.

When Eben first came out of the coma, he seemed to be suffering from amnesia. It seemed all he could remember was his visit to heaven.

It seems that Eben's near-death experience is unique in the fact that since he was a neurosurgeon he knew full well how the human brain functioned.

He had been what was always considered a "scientific reductionist" that believed these experiences people said they had been having was just a product of their brains and that their "consciousness" and "mind" existed separate from their body.

Eben will now tell you that his scientific belief currently is this: "The skeptical scientist that has become addicted to his "scientific simplistic, reductionist" attitude of the world will eventually go away once people realize and open themselves up to what is happening after death.

Eben tells of his experience when he was supposedly "dead." He went on to explain to everyone about being in another realm or world if you will, a sense of peace so deep and abiding that one cannot put it into words, and there is the knowledge you are surrounded by of the presence of such a pure love as you have never experienced before in your life. While in this other world, heaven, he came to know a beautiful girl who sat on a butterfly and accompanied him everywhere. There was no speaking necessary as their thoughts passed back and forth between them without words being needed.

It was several months after the near-death experience, and Eben was still pondering about the beautiful girl and the butterfly. He had never met her in his real life he was sure of that, and that confirmed his theory that his experience was in fact real.

Eben knew he had been given up for adoption when he was only two weeks old. It had been almost a year before he had fallen into his coma when he got to meet with his biological family for the first time in his life. He was introduced to his biological brother, sister, mom, and dad. Unfortunately, he had had a sister, Betsy, younger who had died years earlier.

Eben had gone so far as to have a sketch artist to draw the picture of the young lady riding on the butterfly he had met in heaven. He felt he had to find out who she was as her face haunted him.

It was a while after his coma when his biological family sent him his dead sister Betsy's picture and all of a sudden he knew that the girl he met in heaven was his younger sister who had died.

The stories of those who say they have visited heaven all sound the same over and over and no one knows anyone else, so they have not been able to compare and collaborate. The universal story is always the same; they have never felt such unconditional love as they feel when they are there.

I look forward to the day to be able to enter the kingdom of God. For me, there is no fear of dying. No apprehension comes over me when I think about it. I know my God has plans for me. I believe in His Word and His Promises.

My heart has been heavy at many funerals I have attended as I did not always know the person's relationship with God. I felt unsure about their hereafter. I worried about them. When I would be around them before they passed, I tried to bring up my Christianity and speak to them about salvation.

For those who did not want to talk about it, I would be even more concerned when I attended their funeral. I blame myself and think if I had tried a little harder or made more of an effort when they would change the subject. At the same time, I was always afraid I would push them farther away from God.

So, back to the big question. When is euthanasia the right choice? In my personal, Christian opinion, never, is it the right choice. It is you choosing when you should die and not God who created you.

I only speak the truth as my mind interprets it. Each person does have the right to their opinion and must live and die with their own decisions. You alone must make your choices, but remember, you alone will live eternally with the choice you make.

Chapter 6

When is a DNR The Right Choice?

First, we need to know fully what a 'DNR' is before we discuss it. It means 'Do Not Resuscitate.' The doctors still treat you and take care of the rest of your needs such as antibiotics and fluids, unless you have a living will or advance directive that states otherwise. If your heart or breathing stops, the DNR will keep them from pursuing heroic measures to bring you back to life, and they will allow you to walk into that bright light that so many refer to when they have a near-death experience.

Whatever you do, do not mistake a DNR for euthanasia. They are nowhere the same. You can change your mind about a DNR and reverse it at any time.

It is smartest to think about this ahead of time when you are well. When you are in torment and panic and feeling confused and guilty, you cannot think straight, and it is not the time to make a life or death changing decision.

There are so many different scenarios that can be played out with the DNR.

Most of them having to do with your age, your family situation, your chances of survival, and we should listen to what your doctor's opinion is on your condition at the time.

If the family asks their loved one not to choose DNR but that resuscitation efforts be utilized every time their heart stops beating; in some cases, it is unfair to the patient, no matter how much the family loves them. Ultimately, if the patient is of sound mind, it is the patient's decision.

In the elderly, during the resuscitation process there, unfortunately, comes risks. More times than not there are multiple broken ribs and sometimes punctured lungs. Sometimes our loved ones end up on a ventilator that is breathing for them. You know they do not want to live like that; lying in bed day after day, not knowing anyone or anything with total care being given to them and kept alive by machines.

If you have ever been on a respirator or have been coded, then you can understand the pain your loved one suffers if they are shocking and compressing every few hours trying to keep that patient "alive." They are not alive; they are in a state of "existence." The pain is more than you can imagine. The compression on ribs broken in the prior code causes enough pain to make the patient black out entirely if they are not already in a comatose state.

About 90% of physicians do not want resuscitation or any other form of aggressive treatment and choose to die at home if they are faced with a terminal illness. Doctor's want to have a gentle death because they know that those extraordinary measures have NO meaning. The problem being is that most doctors never talk to their patients about dying.

We wonder why doctors never want to talk about death; it seems it is all left up to the nurses. Shame on the doctors. The doctors tell you that they have never been trained to talk to the patients about dying. They say they have only been taught in prolonging someone's life. This is just nuts. If a patient and his family cannot trust their doctor to be open and honest with them, then who can they trust? Being in healthcare for so long, I back the doctor in the corner and make him answer my questions until I feel I have my money's worth. He better answer every question and tell me the prognosis. It is my right as a patient and I need to know how to prepare for the inevitable.

Doctors feel it is easier to give the patients and their families hope rather than tell them the reality of the situation. Families, in turn, want to grasp at any straw of hope.

Another interesting tidbit that may play a substantial part in this discussion with the patient is that Medicare does not reimburse the doctors to have the end of life talk with their patients.

With there being so many seniors being diagnosed with Alzheimer's now and there being so many stages of the disease and different patients going through the stages at different paces, it makes DNR even more of a consideration for a family who has a loved one in a nursing home or hospice.

Our family ran into a problem with a DNR when a dear grandfather had on his own requested a DNR, and he asked that it be carried out through surgery for which he was scheduled. It is common for most hospitals to suspend the DNR during said operation, but grandpa John had made a special request that the DNR remained during the surgery. It was a simple procedure done under moderate sedation so Grandpa was in and out of it during the procedure. Whoever did not carry out his wishes was where the first error occurred. Then, the doctor should have never talked him into the operation in the first place. It was not needed.

He had been going through months of blood transfusions every two weeks for several months because his bone marrow had shut down and he was not making more blood to survive on his own without the transfusions. He was suffering from myelodysplasia. He was developing antibodies to other donor's blood because of all the blood transfusions he had been exposed to, and the antibodies in them were not playing well with his antibodies making it hard to find compatible donor blood. His lungs had been filling with fluid due to his congestive heart failure, and his breathing was getting worse all the time.

The doctor had been able to convince him and his little elderly wife that if they took him to surgery and did a 'brushing' inside his lungs that he would get better. At that time I was several states away on a business trip, and his daughter who was POA (power of attorney for healthcare) was never contacted about the surgery so she could discuss the possible outcomes with her father.

His little elderly wife, not understanding all the medical jargon and could not hear thunder if it was next to her head agreed with whatever the doctor threw at them, of course, he made them think he would be well in no time. Grandpa couldn't hear either and was too proud to admit it.

During the procedure, something went dreadfully wrong. We reviewed Grandpa's chart later when his daughter arrived and found out the 'something' that went wrong must have ruptured a major artery as he started losing blood rapidly and he immediately coded all the while they kept infusing whatever blood they could grab to give him whether compatible or not.

They did not pay attention to his DNR and kept coding him, but when he came back to his room, he was on a ventilator and never regained consciousness. The sad part was, grandpa knew something was wrong because for some reason he was conscious enough to tell them something was wrong as it was documented in his chart. Those were the last words he ever spoke, and those around him were not to his family.

His wife in her eighties did not comprehend the totality of the situation. He was gone. Grandpa had lost so much blood that his brain had gone without oxygen for far too long, and they had performed a Code Blue on him that he had requested not be done even in surgery. Because of his little wife not understanding the situation, we let him remain on the ventilator for one week so she could grasp that he would not be waking up.

That entire week, she continued to think every day that he would wake up and she would get angry with anyone who tried to explain to her that he probably would not. When the week was over, his daughter who he had named as his POA signed for the ventilator to be turned off and let nature take its course.

Grandma was mad at everyone. If she had been the POA, she would have kept him on the ventilator forever and have family driving her the 90 miles to the hospital every day even though we all worked.

After the ventilator was unhooked, he was able to breathe on his own for a very short period, and his heart continued to beat; both for about 45 minutes after everything had been removed. His heart slowed down a little at a time, and his respirations did the same. There were intervals where he did not take a breath for quite some time, and we would think that it was his last.

I felt so sorry for him and all that he had been put through. An injustice had happened, and he was the victim. He had not deserved anything that had happened to him. It is not what he had signed up for; he had signed up for dying in surgery if it came to it.

He had made peace with his Lord, and at the age of 84, and had been baptized. Bless his heart. He always had the sweetest smile on his face and was so kind to others. It was all so wrong. I was angry for him because he was not 'at himself' to be indignant and outraged to tell the doctor where he stood. His daughter and I, his daughter-in-law had to be his advocates, and when he needed us most, we were both hours away.

No doubt by reading the chart, the surgeon messed up terribly in surgery. He knew he did when we spoke to him. We told him we knew what he had done and that he was the one who had to live with himself. What was worse, he brutalized a little man, killed him, and coded him AGAINST his wishes and then brought him back to his room to exist on a ventilator for what?

To lie for seven days on a ventilator when the doctor already knew he was dead because he had killed him in the operating room from performing an unnecessary procedure on him all for the sake of money. The doctor could only hold his head down in shame.

I know what you are thinking. His daughter and I both being in healthcare wanted to take the doctor to court or have him reprimanded in some way by the medical board, but they would have done nothing, and the lawsuit would not have done a thing as no attorney would have even taken on the case.

A man grandpa's age and with all his health problems was not worth wasting their time and effort. If you factored in the amount of time, he had left on this earth, and what his value was to his wife and society, then he was worth zero.

It did not matter that he had children and grandchildren and great-grandchildren that all loved him to the moon and back. Face it, in the government's eyes; he had lived long enough. He was a burden to society. His value and contribution to the community was nothing. His health as it was, was sucking up valuable resources from the

Medicare system. So his 'value' in court would be the same as it was to society. There was no recourse to make the doctor remember forever what he had done to this little gentle man.

Our only hope is the words we said to him at the time we talked to him. We told him that he was the one who had to live with himself for killing someone outright, against his wishes and all for money as the doctor did not care for Grandpa. He may not have had many days or weeks left, but those few precious days and weeks were his weeks, not the doctors to decide to take away. He had no right to play God.

However, in some cases if you are not careful, Do Not Resuscitate can also be a two-edged sword if in the wrong hands of a family member. Sadly enough, if someone has lived to be almost 100, that means their children are probably close to 80 years old themselves and may not be in good health either. They may be ready for mother or father to check out, and if they are, they might be more than willing to sign a DNR.

In cases like the above, dying is not always so easy. If you still have clarity of mind, and a lot of people now in their 90s and over 100 years old are right on the mark; know what is going on better than you think. They hear what their children are talking about and know full well when they are not wanted. How sad that must be to feel that everyone has quit caring about you, and signed the forms to withhold any further treatment of any kind and to find out your children have signed the DNR.

Be careful who you pick as your power of attorney for health care. Make sure they know your wishes thoroughly and that they love you enough to abide by such.

While I trust my daughter thoroughly, I have still made out my living will so that she will not have to make a decision or be confused with what to do when the time comes. I have only asked to be kept comfortable, no heroic measures taken and to let me die a simple, dignified, pain-free death. Don't keep feeding me through a special tube, don't keep giving me IV's to keep me hydrated, just take care of me and keep me comfortable. By that I mean, keep me at home in my bed and let me die with my loved ones around me. If I don't feel like eating, do not make me eat. Do not make me feel guilty and eat to make you feel better. Let me continue to make my own decisions.

If I want a drink, give it to me if I can drink. If I can't drink, just moisten my lips. If I don't want a drink, then don't force me. That is all I ask. Simple and to the point. When the time comes, let me step out onto Eternity softly to be with my loved ones who have gone on. I will go there and wait for my beautiful daughter to arrive along with her husband and children when their time comes. I will keep their pictures displayed in my mansion and tell my visitors that this is my family I am waiting on. It won't be long before they arrive because time in heaven is only a blink of the eye.

My family and I have always been animal lovers, and we have consistently taken in strays and nursed them back to health, and the Lord help us, we have most of the time kept them unless we found wonderful homes for them or if they were wild creatures we would rehab them and return them back to the wilderness.

When I would lose a beloved pet, I would usually cry for days on end. The first day was racking sobs all day long. I would not eat, and my grieving heart would feel it was breaking. The second day I would cry, but the sobbing had let up. I would eat a little, but not very much. On the third day, I would spend a lot of time in the outdoors and cry when I was outside. By the fourth day, I would only cry when I was alone. And, yes, I cry as I write this as I can remember so many dear pets I have had that have taught me so much about life. Now that I am older, I feel so sorry for my parents because of the child I was when I lived at home. We had so many animals on the farm, and I turned everything into a pet; so there was some farm animal dying all the time, so that made me a constant hot mess.

My father told me that he always felt God put animals on earth for our enjoyment and for us to learn how to grieve when we lost loved ones. I have not been a good student in this area; I can assure you of that. It has not gotten any easier as I have aged. I still cry, only now I cry longer than usual and miss them more deeply since I am an adult. I know my father's wisdom is probably right, but it does not lessen my pain and the missing of my pets.

I have had more pets than I can count in my life and so many I have taken to the veterinarian because they were suffering so terribly that I have asked the veterinarian to put them down due to that fact.

My vet can tell you that every time I ask for his help in this area that I cry for what seems forever, hard racking sobs because I feel like I am acting like God. I feel like I am asking for euthanasia for my pet.

They always leave me to the last appointment of the day. I feel like I am the one deciding as to when my pet dies. Not God, the creator of all creatures of the earth. It bears on me more than anyone can realize. Sounds crazy to some I suppose. Just remember, God knows every sparrow that falls.

Bear with me for a minute while I veer away from the main point.

Don't get me wrong, my veterinarian and his wife are Christians too. They will not put an animal down until it is necessary.   My pets that have had cancer and were suffering and gasping for each breath they took and that I have had to put down have especially broken my heart.

I discussed this situation with my veterinarian, "But, aren't I playing God when I make this decision?" He said, "This pet has been your friend now for years, and they are suffering terribly.   You have a chance to stop that suffering. It is something you can do for your friend who has lived a good life and given you many good years." That is the part that always gets me.

I know that we, as humans have the option of hospice and medications to help us with pain, and we have oxygen to help us breathe without so much effort, but our pets do not have that option.

There are so many people I know and almost every minister except a few who do not believe there will be animals in heaven. Sorry guys, our pets do not have souls but they do have spirits, and when the Lord comes back, the Bible says He will be riding a white horse. Will He not? The last time I read Revelations, it sure said He would be riding a horse. If there are no pets in heaven, where does He get that white horse?

He saved all the animals on the ark, did He not? He gives us pure joy from the creatures He has created and placed here on this earth that He designed for us. From those creatures, by just taking time and paying close attention, we can learn so many things from them. Animals are wise beyond humans in many ways. God has placed in them ways to survive that humans do not have the capabilities of understanding.

Animals are more in tune with what is going on around them than what most people give them credit.

After my grandfather had passed away, he had a little dog named Lucy who pined for him more than anyone could explain. We brought Lucy to live with us and cared for her because she had been around our family the most. It was sad to watch her sorrow and how she mourned for my grandparents. She missed them worse than any animal I had ever been around at the age of sixteen years old.

Lucy developed heart failure and was so weak she could not even go up and down the steps into our home. Each night after midnight she would awaken my father to let her go outside to relieve herself. With congestive heart failure, she was so full of fluid all the time. He would get up and carry her down the steps and wait for her to whine to know to carry her back up the steps. She would be outside for long periods of time, extended periods of time, sometimes even hours.

One night, Dad decided to follow her and see what she was doing outside that kept her so long out of concern for her health. He could not believe his eyes when she went to our family cemetery and lay between Grandma and Grandpa's graves! How could she have possibly known where they were buried? She was not taken to their burial services when they were laid to rest.

The night that Grandpa died, at the exact time he died, she cried a wounded animal cry. My cousin was with her when this happened. Within five minutes my dad called my cousin to tell him Grandpa was gone, that he had crossed over Jordan. My cousin told my Dad that he already knew about it. My cousin told Dad that Lucy had already told him that Grandpa had just died when she wailed that terrible mourning wail.

When Lucy passed away, my Dad dutifully buried her where her heart always had been. Between my grandparent's graves. She was finally back with the two people she had loved more than anything else in the world.

In the winter, you only need to watch the birds outside and when they start feeding voraciously at your bird feeders, and you think they are starving by the way they are eating; they know something you don't. They know that snow or an ice storm is moving in and they are trying to get food before the snow or ice covers up their food supply on the ground.

Who do we depend on for this information? Who else? The weatherman of course who is rarely ever right. Sorry to all those meteorologists out there, but God has placed in His creatures an element of survival that humans do not have.

If God can give this much knowledge to the animals; think of the wealth of experience we have at our fingertips that we never unlock.

We should never settle for less and always work for more than we can get out of life and live each day as our last. Still letting everyone we love know we are thinking about them and letting them know we love them.

Now, sorry to have deviated but getting back to the DNR and Living Will; you will find that most people will not fill this out ever, as they do not want to think ahead to this point of their life; the point when it is the END, the last curtain call.

Nor will they fill out a living will or Health Care Power of Attorney.

Not having a living will, or Health Care POA, or a signed DNR alone can lead to so much bickering and fighting at the deathbed by members of the family because someone in the family will want to stop life support and others will not. I know this as fact because I have witnessed this over and over in my career working in healthcare. It is so unfortunate and leaves so many scars for years to come for the entire family.

They forget that life is a journey and when death comes we change one body for another, and the next body is much better than the one we have now if you are a Christian. Myself, I look forward to getting my thirty-year-old body back. I will be able to run again without pain and have plenty of air in my lungs. The wrinkles that I have earned over the years will be gone!

My new journey will begin, and only happiness will abound for eternity. There will be no bickering and fighting. As the Bible says, we will know them as we knew them. We will know everyone in heaven that we knew on earth. Even if it were someone we didn't enjoy being around on earth, in our heavenly home, it will be wonderful, and there we will enjoy being together.

We will not be sitting on clouds all day strumming our harps if that is what you think. There is always something going on in heaven, and we will be busy all the time. In Heaven, we will not get tired. I can hardly wait for that part. Never get tired. Wow.

No matter what some may try to tell you when you believe in the Lord Jesus Christ, there is a beautiful life for us in heaven when we leave this earth. There is nothing to fear when we close our eyes that last time.

A very dear friend of mine had moved her mother in with her and had her live with her in the last days of her life. Her mother and she both were firm in their faith. Her mother had Alzheimer's, and some days she was very clear in her thinking, and other days she was, well, not so with it.

On the night she died everyone had gone to bed and gone to sleep, but something just woke my friend up from her slumber and told her to go to her mother's bedside. She went in, and everything was fine with her mother, but she pulled up a chair and sat at her bedside and sang softly to her. Her mother was dying from end-stage kidney failure and a long list of other health issues. She had decided she wanted no more dialysis and to go on to be with her husband. She and her daughter would talk a lot about heaven, and she would ask her daughter "tell me what you think it will be like when I get to the gates of heaven?" Her daughter would always answer her the same way. I will be holding your hand here, and when you cross over Jordan, Dad will be standing on the other side with his hand out for you to take it. He will be waiting for you with a big hug. He will be so glad to see you.

Her mother drifted in an out of sleep that night, but something kept my friend at her mother's bedside. My friend sang gospel songs softly to her mother that she knew that her mom liked, and while she was singing to her and holding her hand, her mother took her last breath on this earth and stepped out onto Eternity to meet the prince that she had loved forever.

Should There Be an Obituary About Your Death?

I am sure you think that is a ridiculous question here in the middle of this chapter. It just was not enough to build an entire chapter around, but something to think about and have written up for your children, so they do not have to do it.

When I read an obituary, and some of them are so long it takes up three columns in the newspaper, it makes me sad for the family. It seems to appear that they are trying to prove the person was a righteous person because of all that he/she had accomplished in their lives and how brilliant they were, and they wanted everyone to know he/her was 'Somebody' before they passed away. They made it sound like their works and deeds would get them to heaven as it never listed a church affiliation or their Christianity.

They list all their friends, their children, grandchildren, and great-grandchildren and all their 'special' friends and all of their friends that lived far away. It makes me start wondering if any of them ever came to visit this person while they were alive. Living that far away would be difficult to visit very often and especially if one was in the nursing home.

And how about the obituary that tells every little accomplishment the deceased who is 92 years old had while living down to his merit badge in Boy Scouts? Come on now, is that not a bit much? They tell how they graduated from here, and graduated from there and were chosen for this and were presented with that and the list goes on forever. But, they needed to make up the massive obituary because maybe as the children they felt guilty, or they want to feel important. At least, that is my way of thinking.

Then when I read an obituary that reads only the person's name and no list of relatives and that they will be buried in Potter's Field, it makes me want to weep for those individuals. It means they had no one to mourn their passing and they must have been very alone when they passed from this life.

For myself, I do not want an obituary. I, myself, do not need any of my accomplishments listed during my lifetime. I am not up for a Lifetime Achievement Award at this point in life. My soul will have achieved its reward when I enter Heaven's gates! That is my Lifetime Achievement! That is the Award of a lifetime. Whatever my daughter does beyond my request I have no control over. I feel that I came into this world surrounded by the people who loved me the most, my parents who celebrated me into this world. When I die, if it is the natural course of life, I hope to be surrounded by those I love the most, my daughter, her husband, and my three grandsons. If, in case it is not the natural order of things then add my parents, my dear aunts and my best friend of over 40 years and her two daughters and their families who I always called my nieces. They are the only ones who need to know. Them and well, the crematorium.

I am no great person, nor have I ever been. I have loved my life, and I am celebrating where I am now after death. No need to write a glowing obituary. I had nothing I wanted to prove in my life except to love and be loved by my family. The ones to gather at my deathbed are a part of my heart and will be forever.

Face it; funerals are getting to be something of a burden for most people. The last few funerals I have attended have not had significant attendance at the visitation or the funeral. It is so draining on the family, and they are utterly worn out when it is all over, and the rush of the adrenaline drops so quickly that it is hard to pull one's self out of that physical and mental depression into which you fall.

Funerals have become BIG business. You can estimate the expense of a funeral to be at a minimum of about $6,000, and that is with a cheap casket. The funeral directors get you at your most vulnerable time. They hit you up with all the other extras. The guestbook, the matching thank you cards, the flowers, the necklaces with your loved one's fingerprint, the unique urn for ashes for $1200 that you can buy online precisely like it for $150. There are charges if you have a "visitation" or "wake" the night before the funeral and then there are charges for the "funeral" itself and taking the body to the cemetery. The list can go on and on. Don't get me wrong; I too have been lured into the moment in all this as well. I am just saying; the funeral homes know how to make their money and when to go in for the kill.

One type of funeral that is making a comeback that was popular in 1950 and before is to have the visitation of the deceased in your own home. That is right. To bring the body after it has been embalmed and, in the casket, back to the house and have the visitation where the person lived. To leave the body there all night and let the family take turns sitting with the body until the next day of the funeral. I never fully understood why we got away from this practice.

When my aunt was killed tragically at the age of 20 years old, her body was laid out in the family home where she had lived. She had never been married, and my grandmother had her buried in a white casket, white lining of the coffin, with a white dress. She had been engaged to be married, but her life was cut short before that could happen and I feel that was as close as grandma could come to a wedding for her. I do not know that for a fact, and my father was only five years old, but being on the outside and looking back, it would be the most logical explanation I could pull up in my mind.

What we find today is that the people who attend the funeral are usually the close family and close friends of the family. The wake and funeral is nothing like it used to be because everyone is working. But that is ok, I for one understand.

There are already four funeral homes in the United States that have drive-through visitation for mourners. The drive-through is timed so that it is not at the same time as viewing hours where the family is present. The drive-through has a guestbook, music and a place where you can leave a condolence card.

Some families opt to have visitation and service both late in the afternoon/evening, so more people can attend after work. It is true especially if the family plans on cremation.

I, for one, do not want anyone to have to view my body after I have passed from this world. Gravity is not kind as you lay in the coffin. Everything my body possesses will wither towards my sides, and that will not be a pretty picture. Instead of my usual three chins, in their place there will appear five or six I am sure. And, that does not even start to talk about other areas of the body that will not stand up as they should. A closed casket and a picture of me on top will have to suffice if my daughter must have a service. I prefer a small, intimate, by invitation only graveside service to place my ashes in the ground.

As I said, I was never famous, never planned on being famous, and never felt I was better than anyone else. Therefore, that is why I choose to leave this world as quietly as I came into it. No one would need to buy flowers, bring food by, come to the funeral home, send cards and oh, by the way, there would be a lot of life insurance money left over for my daughter and her family to take a very long vacation to an island somewhere for a few weeks to months. That would make me blissfully happy if they could do that.

As you see, dying does have its rewards. Because of God, there is eternal hope.

Revelations 21:3-4 says, "He will live with them, and they will be His people. God, Himself will be with them. He will wipe every tear from their eyes, and there will be no more death or sorrow or crying or pain. All these things are gone forever."

I am sure you remember when the eight Christian Students were killed in October of 2015 in a college campus shooting because of their beliefs. They were eight students who in the prime of their life and were staunch Christians who took a stand for their Christian views and were unafraid of the consequences; all died knowing full well what would happen to them. They all were unafraid to face their death.

When a real Christian faces death they know it is not hopeless. It is opening the door to start their new life with Christ and to live forever.

A Physicians Perspective on the Crucifixion of Jesus

If you remember, even Jesus was scared as to what was about to happen to him. Mark 14: 32-35 says that before His persecution that at Gethsemane Jesus fell to the ground and prayed that if it was possible for God to please take this cup from me. Not what I will, but what you will.

He was not afraid of why He was doing this, but He was scared of the pain that was to come.

And to revisit that topic, isn't that what most people fear about death? How they will die and that it might be painful?

Have you ever read the medical analysis of Christ's death by crucifixion? Now, that was a form of death that I seriously doubt anyone could top as far as unbearable pain and seemingly never-ending. You would be begging for death.

Before Jesus was to be crucified the next day He did go to the garden of Gethsemane to pray to His Father about the coming day and to beg if there were any way that this could be avoided he would ask that it be so. But He understood that it was God's will. He prayed for a very long time, and He prayed so hard that He sweated so much that His sweat turned to blood and dripped to the ground.

Physicians tell you that it is rare, but yes, this can happen. It is called hematidrosis. It is caused by emotional stress that makes capillaries inside your sweat glands break. It causes the blood to then mix with the sweat.

When Jesus was arrested a soldier stepped forward and hit Him in the face because Jesus would not speak up. Then, after He was blindfolded, they kept hitting Him in the face and spitting on Him.

Early the next morning Jesus who was already beaten up, bruised and exhausted, dehydrated and had not slept all night long was drug before Pontius Pilate. They took off all Jesus's clothes and took His hands and pulled them above His head and tied them to a post. The Romans made what they called a flagellum which was a whip that had many leather strips attached to it and at the end of two of the pieces were balls of lead. The Romans started beating Jesus on His back all the way down His buttocks and His legs. It caused the skin of His back to be torn to shreds, and there was arterial bleeding from His back from the muscles.

They kept making fun of Him as 'King of the Jews' and took thorn limbs to make a crown and jammed it on His head causing bleeding. They took a stick and hit the crown, so it slammed down harder on His head causing even more bleeding.

Jesus, in shock, was not even able to carry the massive wooden beam of His cross. Simon of Cyrene carried it, and Jesus walked behind Him all the time bleeding. They took off all of Jesus's clothes again except His loincloth. He refused the wine they offered. Jesus was thrown against the cross where the Roman drove the nails through His wrists and into the wood. The Roman then placed one foot on top of the other and hammered a nail through both feet and into the wood.

It was then that Jesus sagged with all the weight hanging on the nails on His wrists. It had to have caused excruciating pain to shoot up His arms and explode inside His brain. When His arms became so fatigued, the cramps began in His muscles causing terrible, throbbing pain. His pectoral muscles then became paralyzed. He could get a little air into His lungs, but He could not get it out. Because of all of this, the carbon dioxide got higher in His bloodstream and inside His lungs.

At times He pushed Himself up, so He could exhale to get a little bit of oxygen. It is thought it was during these times He whispered some of His last words.

When He saw the soldiers trying to win his clothes He said: "Father, forgive them for they do not know what they do."

To the thief: "Today, thou shalt be with me in Paradise."

When He looked down at his mother: "Woman, behold your son." Then He looked at His brother John and said: "Behold your mother."

His fourth cry was: "My God, My God, why have You forsaken Me?"

His pericardium started filling with fluid and was compressing His heart and causing a terrible crushing pain in His chest.

The end of His life was coming on fast now. His heart was so compressed and barely able to pump because what blood there was, was so thick and heavy, He could scarcely gasp small bits of air. Jesus gasped out: "I thirst."

Someone had taken a sponge and dipped it in some cheap wine and pressed it to His lips. Jesus could feel the sting of death running through His body. With barely a whisper He said: "It is finished." "Father, into Your hands I commit My spirit."

It was customary for the soldiers to break the leg bones of the victims but when they got to Jesus, they saw that they didn't need to do anything. But, to make sure He was dead, they took a spear and drove it up through His ribs and into the pericardium and the heart.

Physicians feel that Jesus died of heart failure because of shock and the fact that the heart was so constricted by the fluid in the pericardium.

I cannot imagine a death such as this. I cannot in my mind think of any manner of death that could be as horrendous as this death. There may be a torture worse than this, but I cannot imagine such.

In today's world, we have medicines available to help keep our pain controlled and to help us through the hard times. There was nothing during Jesus's time that would work to dull the pain. The nasty wine they gave was not enough to make any man drunk enough to keep from feeling any pain.

Chapter 7

Is Cremation Wrong?

As I have bared my heart on many subjects in this book, I also want you to think about the 'after' of death. Why? Because you must think about death ahead of time and you should do so as a responsible person so that your children and loved ones know what you want to have done after you have breathed your last.

No scripture in the Bible gives direction on what and how to bury someone. Over the years, burial practices have changed significantly. In Jesus's day, they used spices and oils to wash the body with and wrap with a shroud before entombment.

In ancient times of Israel, they felt the body had to be buried on the same day. The Egyptians embalmed their dead as to delay the decaying process and prepare them for their afterlife.

Today, if someone chooses burial, they are embalmed with a solution of partial formaldehyde to delay the decaying process, so the family will have time to mourn their loved one.

Our culture on burial is rapidly changing, however. Since funerals are getting more and more expensive, you find families more and more are turning to cremation. As I mentioned in another chapter of some of the funeral costs incurred to bury a loved one, there are other things that you must add in as well. You also have to pay the minister, buy a burial plot, hire gravediggers, and closers, find pallbearers, purchase a tombstone, hope it is not raining the day you lay your loved one to rest, and whether or not you want to buy an expensive vault to be placed in the ground to hold the casket.

Just remember these words as we have all heard them: "Dust to dust, ashes to ashes."

It seems that some families worry that when Jesus returns in the Rapture and the bodies of those who believe in Christ arise from the dead that maybe there will not be anything there to resurrect if it is ashes. What does it matter, for those who have been dead for hundreds of years, they have already turned back to dust anyway? God is big enough to take a speck of dust and bring forth a body believe me. He formed Adam in the Garden of Eden from the clay of the earth.

Some families like to make visits to a cemetery and place flowers. That is all fine and good. Let us remember, however, that person is no longer 'there.' (If we are absent the body, we are present with the Lord; 2

Corinthians 5:8).   You are visiting a tombstone and memories. There is nothing wrong with that I can assure you. If you are like me, it brings comfort and solace. I, like most people, find myself talking to my loved one that has passed. They cannot hear me, but it makes me feel better. I know God hears me and maybe He will get my message through to my loved one, and if not, God will know the condition of my heart.

You can find nothing in the Bible that refutes cremation. I know some of the older generations do not like cremation, and I think it is because it reminds them of the fires of hell. That is not so. It is merely a way to dispose of our human remains.

The human body is composed almost totally of water. When the cremation is complete, about all that is left is the bones. The crematorium takes the bones and grinds them up very fine, so they take on the look of ashes.

Every living cell of our body that God breathed life into is composed almost entirely of water. That in and of itself is pretty much a miracle. My skin right now does not look like it, but it too is made of water.

Some put them in a pretty urn and set Mom and Dad on their fireplace with their picture on the front. Others sprinkle them out over their favorite place; like the land they bought and lived on. Then there is the person who requests to have his ashes spread out over a lake or the ocean. Each person has their own choice of what they want to be done with their ashes when they have passed away.

I have told my parents, my Aunt, and Uncle I will keep their ashes on my mantle and I will talk to them and tell them about what happens every day. I will have them with me all the time if I travel somewhere. We laugh at the thought of me traveling with urns. Of course, I will not be doing that, but I will be cherishing the moments I have had with each of them by having their ashes nearby on my fireplace mantle. I do not care what other people think of me. I have always been that way, forged my path and never felt I had to follow the crowd. I am God's unique design, and He has made me as I am.

I do not want to take the chance that one day someone comes along and decides to take over the land where the cemetery lies now to build something there. They promise you in the contract that the bodies will be exhumed and moved with the tombstones. That is not the truth. Therefore, another reason to be cremated, better than seeing your loved one's coffin float by during a flood while new construction is taking place where a cemetery once stood. It happens more than you can imagine.

How do I know this? I had a cousin who worked in construction in California who helped move a cemetery, and all they moved was the tombstones. Not one body was exhumed. He said it was terrible and he felt horrible about being a part of it.

Chapter 8

What Happens After We Are Buried?

What does happen to us after we are buried and when we are six feet below in the dirt with or without a vault. It is only our flesh after all. Our soul has left us and is either in heaven or hell.

Does it matter at this point?

We have lived our life, and from dust, we were designed, and to dust, we shall return.

So many people get worried about what happens "after" the dirt is thrown upon their casket. When there is no chance for you to get out and escape this horror of the unknown; it does not matter at this point as you have made your choices in life as to how it will all turn out. There are those who worry that there will be worms that will come along and help their body with the decaying process.

Some are afraid of the dark and go so far as to have a battery supplied light placed in the casket with them. I am sure at this point, there is no sound reasoning for the flashlight and whether it is dark or not inside your coffin is the least of your worries.

You might be surprised to know that you will not start to decompose where it is visible before 4-7 months. It is all dependent on what climate you have been buried in if your casket has been placed in a vault.

At this point, the embalming fluid will start seeping out of your body as you decompose, and your skin starts showing breaks and holes.

The fluid draining from you will seep out and collect in the bottom of the casket and from there flow down to the cement vault. The time frame for all of this is about 1-2 years.

There is something like a waxy white substance that aggregates on the parts of your body that has fat in it, and it is called adipocere or "grave wax." The areas you usually see this in are the abdomen, cheeks, buttocks, and breasts. It is caused by a chemical reaction where the fats in the body start to react with hydrogen and water while in bacterial enzymes. It then breaks down into nothing but soaps and fatty acids. This adipocere is bacteria resistant and can protect the corpse, slowing down the decomposing process. The forming of the adipocere starts to form in about four weeks after you have died and has been found on bodies that have been dug up 100 years later. Now, if the body is easily accessed by insects, you are not likely to see adipocere form.

It is a rare situation, but this can happen and it's simple to understand. If you place a body in a sealed casket, sometimes the gases from the corpse as it decomposes start to get trapped; the pressure will begin to rise and "bam" before you know it, the casket is an exploding balloon. It may not "explode," but all the nasty fluids will boil out with the gases that have been trapped inside as well.

In and around the area of Mount Everest that people call "The Death Zone" there have been well over 200 climbers that have died. Since the conditions, there are so harsh, and there is such a lack of oxygen, you will find that most of those bodies still are on Mount Everest in the very position they were in when they died. On top of that, a majority of the bodies have become mummified due to the sub-freezing weather.

Rigor Mortis seems to be one of the most talked-about signs of death on all the detective shows. It is when the dead persons have their legs or arms stretched out spread-eagle, and their mouth might open grotesquely, but it still happens even though we do not wish to be remembered that way. Can you imagine anything that would be any creepier than walking upon a person that has gone "stiff?"

Would it not be creepy if the dead body stiffened up at the exact moment you died? A cadaver spasm seems to leave a lot of people looking so scary if that happens. It is a rare happening, but it does happen if the person dying faces death that is very violent and occurs to be accompanied by intense physical exertion.

Some of the things that are seen by pathologists, criminal investigators, are so freakish that they make us wish to die peacefully in our sleep.

This is the part of death that we are NOT involved in; we are no longer in this physical body. Our pain and suffering is over, and we have either entered the gates of heaven or hell to live out eternity. We no longer need our physical body so it might as well return to the dust from which it came, to begin within the Garden of Eden.

Chapter 9

Are You Ready for Your Final Goodbye?

Everyone should be ready at any time. We never know when we will take that big final step into "Eternity." I have seen it every day in my work career. I have watched it on my father's face when he has been so ill with his chronic lymphatic leukemia. He is tired, he has fought the good fight, and he is ready to go on to heaven and see his son who died tragically, to see his mother and father who died and that he loved so very much. To see his sister, that was killed in a tragic car accident when he was five, but he does not remember her.

But, for the selfish person that I am, I am screaming inside for him to get better. To try a little harder, I still need my father. He is my closest friend. I am his little girl. I will always be his girl. My heart will genuinely break the day he crosses over Jordan. I am not even sure my heart will ever be able to beat again. The same will be with my mother and my beloved aunt. Our family has such a deep abiding love that it surpasses the kind of love that I see with other families as they do not know what they are missing and it must be sad for them. I have been so very blessed.

I know when the next day comes after any one of them crosses over Jordan that I will awake and my world will have still been shattered. I will not want to get out of bed. The birds will still be singing; the earth will still be rotating. I will wish the day before had never happened. I know I will see them again, but it will seem like forever to me. For my Dad, waiting for us to come to heaven will only be a blink of the eye. The sights he will see in heaven will be so amazing he will hardly be able to wait for the rest of us to join him. He is just that way, he wants to share happy times with his family.

Yes, agnostics and atheists, and those who hold us as the "deplorables," I do hold on to that promise that my Bible gives me. The Bible has proven correct on everything that it has been challenged about over the centuries. The Bible has proved timeless in our World's History. The time shall come when every knee shall bow, and every mouth shall confess that indeed He is Christ the Lord. For some, it will be too late, and you will burn in an eternal lake of fire and brimstone.

But I do believe in my true fairy tale of a Bible, with its beautiful happy ending.

It is so traumatic to some; while there are those who seem to have no empathy and it never seems to affect them.

When my mother's father died, I celebrated for him. I was happy because he did not have to listen to my grandmother nag at him anymore. That is all she had ever done for their entire fifty-something years of marriage was nag at the poor man day and night in her shrill voice.

When my mother's mother died, I never shed a tear because she was one of the meanest, vilest women I had ever known. She was always extremely mean, to my brother and I. We lived the closest and were the handiest. I have not known anyone like her since. I pray that she was like that due to a mental condition.

I always dreaded going to her house because this grandmother was so abusive to me verbally and physically when there was no one around to watch. She ruined my self-esteem for years. I could not bring my adult self to tell anyone what she had done to me until I was 40 years old.

I also knew that it was a big "show" she put on at my grandfather's funeral when she played her grand finale of a performance by asking for a step stool, so she would be tall enough to give him one last kiss on his lips.

Grandma had cheated on my grandfather for years, and everyone at the funeral knew it. Grandpa knew all about her cheating ways and always turned his head and kept staying with her. He told the kids when they got older that he only stayed married to her because of his children.

There are so many things we must suffer through in this life to reach that heavenly rest. The worst of these seem to me to be heartache that others cause us. Such intense despair that we feel our hearts will not be able to beat again on its own without those we love.

I can remember being bullied in school so severely that I thought I might die. I was in first grade, and a fifth-grade girl came into the bathroom when I had just finished and was washing my hands. I did not know the girl. I was a "wittle kid" as my grandson used to pronounce it and shy with hair in pigtails. The larger girl, named Marsha had come over to me, grabbed my pigtails and slammed my head multiple times into the faucet of the ceramic sink and then walked out of the bathroom.

I did not even know this girl. I had no idea why she had done this to me. I was terrified to go to the bathroom after that day. I had the most terrible headache I had ever had in my life up to that point. She had to have busted my head in because it hurt so badly. Why would anyone torture someone they did not even know and what was the purpose? I felt I had faced pure evil at the age of six years old. She never said a word to me. She just abused me and left.

I do not know why kids have to be so mean to others and bully them. There were bullies back when I was a kid, and I never knew what a bully was until the word was brought out and discussed openly in the past few years. It was terrible.

What the reality is, when you grow up and get into the working world, there are just as many bullies there as anywhere else. They are just disguised differently. They mock you behind your back, they lie to your face, they say one thing and mean another, they stab you in the back and then turn the blade when you least expect it, they do everything they can to make sure you do not fit in, they want to make you feel uncomfortable so that you will finally leave your work environment and if they are lucky you will leave the entire company.

You cannot trust anyone you work with as they are all doing their best to grapple their way to the top or just hang on by their fingernails. I have never seen that many people in my life in one place that do nothing but lie to your face.   You are sometimes given tasks that have nothing to do with your job only to see if you will fail.

I have gone through life with some of my cousins disliking me, and I have never understood why. We were poor growing up but I never knew it at the time, and my cousins always thought they were better than my brother and I, but time soon told they were not any better. Their father had to file bankruptcy from farming. They still treated us like we were not worthy people and they were heads above our family.

I knew this was not correct when I graduated as third in the class of 110 students. One of them acted like I was some type of uneducated fool while he barely scraped by with his high school diploma.

His sister, who seemed to think she was much better than I and never had the time of day for me, ignored me when I was around. I tried my best to start small talk with her, but it never went anywhere. Again, I do not know why she disliked me. I wish I did so I could apologize as to why I had made her life so miserable by being around her. She had never been a happy person, and she never seemed to be able to smile, even today. I was one grade behind her in high school and was good friends with all her close friends and got along with all of them exceptionally well.

I can remember at my parent's 25th wedding anniversary celebration when I was laughing with someone about something when she came up to me and said, "Why do you have to always be so happy?" What in the world did that mean? She has never changed to this day.

She did have a younger sister though that seemed to be down to earth and never act better than anyone else. The younger sister was kinder to others and did not treat people like mud on her boots.

Their mother taught them all these exceptional characteristics, or so her older sister thinks. She married young, got pregnant and cried for the entire nine months. I understand she stole money from her parents to buy things for herself. Not always real honest. After the baby was born, a little boy, she divorced her first husband and remarried.   This man hated her son from her first marriage and was not kind to him.

One night, the sister brought the five-year-old son home to her parents and handed him over to her mother and father and said, "There you can have him, I don't want him anymore." The grandparents raised the young man and sent him to college, and he became a journalist and newspaper editor in Texas.

The sad part was, none of her children by her second husband could stand their half-brother. They never wanted to take any time with him. His mother never wanted to make any time for him. They felt like he was only in the way when he came home for a visit with his family, and it caused a lot of arguments amongst his half brother and sisters.

His mother was not a nice person, but she always tried to act to others like she was a kind and caring person out in the community. Trying to put on a front to make everyone think that she was a great mother to him, but that was never true. He always felt that his Aunt was his real mother. She always made time for him, and she always helped him out financially when he developed pancreatic cancer.

When he passed away from "the cure" for pancreatic cancer, guess who rushed down for the funeral? All his half-brothers and sisters and his biological mother who never really had anything to do with him and who didn't even like him before he died. What would he have thought? But, this would make them look good to those he had worked with and maybe get their pictures in the paper.

But, to him, his one aunt who really counted as a mother figure to him was too ill to attend. The funny thing about it was that the biological mother never did tell her sister that he had died. The aunt had kept asking about him because she could not reach him on the phone and was trying to find out how to contact him and his biological mother never told her anything. The aunt had to find out from her brother, my father who was talking about his death one day because he thought she already knew.

I tell you these stories from my life not to run anyone down. I reveal them to you because I want everyone to understand that even though we are Christians, we live life like everyone else, we still face day to day trials and troubles. We still experience the hurts in life. We make mistakes every day. No one is perfect even if they are Christian. You try every day to be a good Christian, but we are still flawed and have a sinful nature no matter what others want to say. Thank goodness we have a loving, forgiving God.

It seems that for the past three years I have been losing loved ones left and right. As a Christian, all of them I know I will see again. But my heart is still so saddened only by my greed for not having them here on earth and being left with only the memories. Something I hold so dear to my heart.

When it comes to facing my death, I do not feel fear. Every time I have had to face death; I have been embraced by such a perfect calm as nothing I have ever felt again. An "existence" of peace that cannot be expressed to anyone unless they have experienced it.

I have a precious little aunt who died at home in hospice care from kidney failure and heart disease. She had been in the hospital, and when they finally took her off the ventilator, she still could not speak for the remaining three weeks of her life because of the damage the ventilator had done to her throat and vocal cords. She looked at her only daughter and said softly, "Home."

I know where she went when she left this earth. Heaven awaited her with open gates and the arms of the angels. She was precious to so many. She and her daughter were extremely close, and her daughter will have a vast void to fill since losing her mother. But she will not regret putting her life on hold for this past year and taking care of her mother and being by her side all the time. There will be memories they have built that will last until they are rejoined in heaven.

If I knew I was to be faced with a terminal diagnosis that the doctors told me would have some terrible issues to face toward the end stages, I know for a fact that God would help me through it, that He would sustain me with His grace to endure whatever I had to go through and help the doctors know what to do to help ease my suffering as much as possible and when my time came to cross over Jordan and step out into Eternity I know I could let go of my loving families hands and reach for my loved ones waiting for me on the other side of the shore. Finally, in the arms of Jesus.

I will go to live my eternal life with my Father in Heaven and all those from Earth that I knew that have gone before me; I will know them as I knew them on Earth when I get to Heaven. The only difference is they will be younger, they will have their health back, no one will ever be sad, no one will ever have a reason to cry, no one will ever have to feel pain anymore, and I will have victory in Jesus!

The people who always hurt me and bullied me, they will be nice now. They will no longer harbor hate in their hearts. I do not understand the hate. Everyone in heaven will be able to get along. That will be such a wonderful time!

I know I will be the happiest I have ever been; to see the face of Jesus and God the Father as I walk the streets of gold. I will be with my family that has gone on before me and with all my pets from over the years.

Chapter 10

How About Those Who Die Alone?

You can probably tell by the way I write that I worry about everyone. I worry about the people who will die alone and by themselves. About the people who have no children or those who have outlived all their family and will be without anyone when they die, and it breaks my heart.

I feel it is so important that someone in the family be present when their beloved family member steps out into eternity. That someone in their family is holding their hand and telling them it is ok to go on, we will be fine, and they were the best mother or father in the world, and you could have never asked for more. They can leave this world without any burdens and enter heaven to see all their loved ones waiting for them there.

I knew of a young man who was working on a construction site and he was the last to leave for the day. He made a misstep on the building he was leaving from and fell to his death on a brick wall below. He was not found until the next morning by his co-workers. I am sure he never knew anything. Yet, he died alone.

There is the young man who had his whole life in front of him and was engaged to be married. He was up in a helicopter to get a good story for the local newspaper. The helicopter crashed killing the pilot immediately. The young man was brought to the emergency room and talking to all the nurses and saying over and over and over, "I'm not going to die am I?" The nurses reassuring him he was not and all the time knowing he was going to die. They could not pump blood into him as quickly as he was bleeding it out. He never got to say goodbye to his parents or his fiance.

My heart is heavy for the elderly who are in the nursing homes who die alone. Those who have no family left, no one to come sit with them as they cross over Jordan. Those who are alert enough to know they are dying and they are doing it all alone. It is utterly heartbreaking.

There are some places in the United States that now have Death Doulas like they have Birth Doulas. A Death Doula is a person trained to sit with someone who is dying and to be with them when they pass on or transcend if you will to their heavenly life.

There are patients who are brought into the Emergency Room that are dying as they are brought in and will be dead within a few hours. Most know they are dying because they know of their diagnosis. Every breath is a gasp.

A gentleman comes in to the ER, he is frightened as he knows he is dying. He is not afraid of dying, it is his suffering from lack of oxygen that is causing him to feel fear.

When asked if he has family to call, he replies that he only has his mother and she is in her 90s and he does not want her to see him like this in the throes of dying. The doctor stays with the patient as long as he can until the Emergency Room is so backed up that he can no longer sit with this dying man that has wrenched his heart tonight. A nurse comes to sit with the dying patient and holds his hand.

The patient is given morphine, not enough to kill him, the doctor knows that would be wrong, but enough to ease his pain of gasping for breath. The patient suffers from a disease that is rare but has hardened all the veins and vessels in his lungs and not allowing any blood exchange to carry oxygen to his lungs. He is dying slowly as the nurse sits and holds his hand.

The nurse sits with the patient in the middle of a busy Emergency Room because they cannot get him to a private room in time for him to die in a quiet place. The patient breathes slower and slower until he finally breathes his last. The physician comes back and marks the exact time of death as 01:32 a.m. He is gone, the nurse is crying. This man, dying alone without his family at his side has saddened her more than words can explain.

It happens everyday in Emergency Rooms all over the world, on mountainsides to climbers who misstepped, to Nursing Home patients that are not found until later dead in their wheelchair or bed, elderly who have been neglected by their family and left to die in their own homes because no one checked on them, and the homeless who are never identified so family can never be located.

Sometimes, the terminally ill patient may have a family, but still, have a Doula because the family is having difficulty dealing with the impending death of their loved one.

The Doula gets to know the terminal patient and finds out how they want to spend the last days of their life. If it means helping them get final papers in order, memory book, audio recordings and other items they might want to pass on down after they are gone.

The Doula will be able to help the family understand the stages of dying as the loved one enters the last part of their life. They will explain it in such a way that the family should be able to see the dying process is wonderful in the eyes of the beholder.

As more and more Americans choose to die in their own homes in their beds, there are more and more requests for Death Doulas. The Death Doulas get such a blessing from serving these terminal patients. They can see families that heal some old wounds, forgiving old transgressions, and new bonds forged that seem to help the dying in their final transition in such a peaceful manner and for those left living to bring new opportunities.

For those who have been terminally ill and had near-death experiences and shared their stories, it will amaze you to find out that when they "visited" what they felt was the heavenly realm, that religion was no barrier when the other religions also believed in God as the one and only creator and that His son died on the cross for their sins. I know every religion believes that their faith is the only true religion, but we must be accepting of what has been seen and experienced and how far-reaching God's love extends and how overwhelming and pure His love is and feels.

Everyone who had a near-death experience talks about the overwhelming and pure feeling of the great love they feel in the heavenly realm. They do not want to return to this earth of sin and hatred. But if it is not their time, they are usually turned back by their family and told it is not your time. Go home.

Near-death experiences have been happening for years now, but many have been so afraid to speak about it and have been scoffed at by physicians. Physicians are now finding that this is happening as some of them have experienced this phenomenon. People's lives are being completely changed due to these experiences.

People who profess that they were atheists and have had near-death experiences come back and give their hearts to God and proclaim Him as Lord and Savior. None of the atheists are embarrassed to tell their stories of their experiences. They are ready to share with the world how their life has been changed, and it was done so by God the Father.

My life was changed at nine years old. I have grown as a Christian, and with each close call to death, I have become closer to God.

I used to keep a prayer list in my day runner that I carried. When the prayer was answered, I would cross it out in yellow. One day while looking back on my prayer list I noticed that everything I had prayed for was marked out in yellow. Why was I keeping a list? I had only proved to my self that God answered every prayer that I had prayed. What a mighty God we serve.

There are some days you feel that God's spirit is so overflowing in you that you are about to burst. You know He has plans for you.

Because I suffer from PTSD from my car wreck, most of my issues revolve around any of my family who is driving, especially long distances or if I have to travel far. When I know my daughter and her family have to go a long distance, I always pray that God sends His tallest guardian angels to surround their vehicle and protect them all while traveling and bring them back home safely to us.

Many wait for the sting of death but the Bible tells us in I Corinthians 15: 55-56: "Where, O death, is your victory? Where, O death, is your sting?" The sting of death is sin and the power of sin is the law (of Moses). Verse 57 goes on to say: But thanks to God! He gives us victory through our Lord Jesus Christ.

That victory he refers to is the victory of living with Him eternally in Heaven in the mansions He has prepared for us.

We must not forget to thank God for each day of our life He so freely gives us and the fact that we wake up every morning. We need to be grateful and thankful for what God does in our lives and the fact that He has gone before us to prepare our mansion in the sky.

If we sat down and listed all the things we had to be thankful for, we would never be done writing the list. My God is WONDERFUL! I am not afraid of the Valley of the Shadow of Death.

Final Words

Birth and death are both magical and finely orchestrated events in one's life. One is opening and coming to life from the womb and all parts of the babies' body becoming independent of the mother, no longer needing her lifeblood.

While death, closes gradually, one part at a time even while other parts try to take over and save the day. Each part of the organ system is dependent on the other and as they shut down, they shut down systematically. How magnificently we have been designed!

Who, but a loving God could have designed such a perfect specimen as the human body that is designed as we are and made up mostly of water. Who, but a loving God could make each of us unique and different from everyone else so that there are no two people alike anywhere in the world.

Death is not to be feared if you are properly prepared. Death is just passing from this life into the next chapter of your life to eternity. Eternity being the most important chapter.

One last thing.

I want to give you a **one-in-two-hundred chance** to win a **$200.00 Amazon Gift card** as a thank-you for reading this book.

All I ask is that you give me some feedback, so I can improve this or my next book.

Your opinion is *super valuable* to me. It will only take a minute of your time to let me know what you like and what you didn't like about this book. The hardest part is deciding how to spend the two hundred dollars! Just follow this link.

http://reviewers.win/dyingwell